**Coursebook**

# Touché !
## En ville à Québec

**4**

PEARSON
Heinemann

Judy Comley

Sydney, Melbourne, Brisbane, Perth, Adelaide
and associated companies around the world

*Touché ! 4* is the fourth stage of Pearson Heinemann's semester-based series in French.
Visit the **Touché !** website at **pearson.com.au/schools/secondary/touche**

**Pearson Heinemann**
An imprint of Pearson Australia
(a division of Pearson Australia Group Pty Ltd)
20 Thackray Road, Port Melbourne, Victoria 3207
PO Box 460, Port Melbourne, Victoria 3207
www.pearson.com.au/schools

Copyright © Pearson Australia 2009
(a division of Pearson Australia Group Pty Ltd)
First published 2003 by Heinemann

2012   2011   2010   2009
10   9   8   7   6   5

Commissioned by Eileen Sedunary and Katie Barnett
Edited by Katie Barnett with Carolyn Glascodine and Amber Parkinson
Points de référence compiled by Philip Bryan
Text design by Marta White
Cover design by Marta White
Illustrations by St2 Creative, Melissa Webb, Boris Silvestri
Photography in Quebec and France by Bill Comley
Additional photography in France by Sue and Malcolm Barnett
Maps by Guy Holt
Teaching consultants: Alice Bray, Kelly Farrell, Catherine Willoughby
Language consultant: Lydie Pradier

Prepress and film separations by Splitting Image Colour Studios, Australia
Printed in China (SWTC)

National Library of Australia cataloguing-in-publication data:

Comley, Judy, 1946–
    Touché ! 4 En ville à Québec: Coursebook.

    For secondary school students
    ISBN 978 1 74085 050 6.

    1. French language – Textbooks for foreign speakers –
    English. I. Title.

448.2421

Pearson Australia Group Pty Ltd    ABN 40 004 245 943

**Acknowledgements**
The author wishes to acknowledge the warmth and generosity
of the Québécois people who in so many ways contributed to
this book. Particular thanks to Chris Leenhouts, Sylvie Carrier,
their sons Ryan and Dominic, and Jacques and Martine Genest for
their hospitality and cultural and linguistic insights. Thanks also to
Annie Lalanne for her help with Québécois expressions. Further
thanks to those people in Quebec and France who generously
allowed photographs, especially to the principal and students of
Collège Victor Hugo in Besançon.

The publishers wish to thank Aventures Nord-Bec who kindly gave
permission to reproduce the photos of the sled dogs on page 35.

Every effort has been made to trace and acknowledge copyright.
The publisher would welcome any information from people who
believe they own copyright to material in this book.

# Contents

# Contents

# Introduction

**En ville à Québec** – stage 4 of the *Touché !* series – takes you across the equator back to the northern hemisphere, to the French-speaking province of Quebec, in Canada. Although far from France and New Caledonia, Nick is soon at home in this part of the Francophone world and eager to discover its features and differences.

Each of the four units in this *Coursebook* has the following sections:

## Learn how to

On the first page of each unit, **Learn how to** lists the main things you'll be able to do by the end of the unit. **Learn about** highlights points of cultural interest that will also be explored. Take some time to look at the photographs – they will give you a preview of what's coming and a chance to make some observations about different aspects of life in Quebec.

## Cartoon story

Meet Nick's new friends – Chloé, her brother Hugo, and her high-spirited friend, Rita. Share Nick's new cultural experiences of Halloween and ice hockey. Join him as he finds his way through the winding streets of the historic walled city of Quebec and discover the language you will need to communicate in similar situations. When you understand all that is happening in the cartoon story, practise imitating the voices on the *Audio CDs* until you are ready to perform the story with some classmates.

## Points de prononciation and Vocabulaire

The **Points de prononciation** remind you that although French and English use the same alphabet, and share many words, the pronunciation can be quite different. The explanations and examples will help you to develop a good accent and also to spell French words correctly. When you can confidently pronounce the new words and expressions listed in the **Vocabulaire** section, use the **Comment dit-on … ?** activity in your *Workbook* to work out their meanings. The word groupings are a useful clue and will also help you to learn the different types of words and their functions.

## En un mot

This page provides you with some extra vocabulary to give you greater scope when talking about the different unit themes. By working with a partner, you will soon become skilled at using these new words in practical conversational situations.

## Verbalisez !

Here you will learn more about different types of verbs and find some entertaining ways to memorise them. Brainstorm ideas from the whole class to write your own **Chant de la tribu**. It's a fun way to develop your oral skills and revise what you've learned.

## Points de langue

This section explains the main language points introduced in each unit's cartoon story. The clear explanations will help you understand how the French language works. They will also allow you to compare and better understand your own language. These new language points will be practised in the listening, reading and writing activities in the *Workbook*. In the *Coursebook*, you'll practise them orally through the following speaking sections.

## Dialogue and Jeu de rôle

By this point, you should be confidently imitating the cartoon story characters (including the narrator) on the *Audio CDs*. The **Dialogue** provides further speaking practice but gives you some choice in what you say within secure guidelines. It also provides helpful ideas for when you are later creating your role-play. The **Jeu de rôle** is the final stage of your oral work and gives you the opportunity to create something of your own from the French you've learned. Use your imagination. Give your characters a personality, dress up, bring props, use gestures and expression to convey meaning – think about not only *what* to say, but *how* to say it – and make your performance for the class as entertaining as possible!

## Connexion culturelle

These pages explore points of cultural interest and will deepen your understanding of the world around you. Find out how this part of Canada came to be French-speaking; learn about Quebec's famous sled-pulling huskies; compare town life in France and Canada; discover what **une poutine** is. You'll find plenty of material for class discussions about what we share with other cultures and how we differ, as well as an interesting variety of extra reading in French.

## À faire

As in *Touché ! 1*, *2* and *3*, up to this point the various sections in each unit are presented in the order you would do them (although your teacher may decide to vary the order to suit your class). However, **À faire** presents a choice of activities for use any time you are looking for something to do – when your teacher is away or when you have finished your work early.

## Appendices and Points de référence

At the end of this *Coursebook*, the **Appendices** section contains a summary of all the regular and irregular verbs learned so far, and some helpful hints on how to use a bilingual dictionary. It also contains a glossary of numbers, colours, days of the week, months and seasons.

This is followed by the **Points de référence** – French–English and English–French vocabulary lists with all the words and expressions used in this *Coursebook*, plus a lot of useful vocabulary from *Touché ! 1*, *2* and *3*.

But it's now time to see how Nick is settling into Quebec. **Bonne continuation !**

# Rencontres

## Learn how to:

- Describe someone's eyes, hair and build
- Say who someone looks like
- Introduce someone
- Make comparisons
- Use –re **verbs**

## Learn about:

- Québec: **Canada's French-speaking province**
- **Some** québécois **history**
- **The people of** Québec
- **Québécois French**

## Je te présente mon copain

À Québec, dans l'appartement de Nick et de son père …

Nick, tu réponds au téléphone ?

DRIIING ! DRIIING !

Allô … Oui, c'est bien Nick Mondine …
Ah oui ! Suzanne, ma sœur, correspond
avec ton frère. Bonjour, Chloé ! …
Oui, ça va très bien … Où ? À la Porte
Saint-Jean ? D'accord … À quatorze heures.
Euh, attends ! Tu es comment ?

Euh … j'ai les cheveux blonds, raides
et mi-longs … Et je porte un pull orange
et un jean bleu. Et toi, tu es comment ?

Michel Cadrin
PHARMACIEN

D'accord ! À la
Porte Saint-Jean
à deux heures,
alors.

Ben … je suis assez grand et
mince. J'ai les cheveux noirs
et raides et les yeux marron.

C'est le correspondant
de Suzanne ?

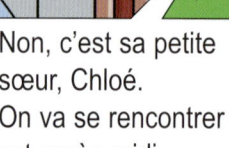

Non, c'est sa petite
sœur, Chloé.
On va se rencontrer
cet après-midi.

*Une heure plus tard, Nick arrive à la Porte Saint-Jean. Il cherche Chloé … La fille là-bas a les cheveux blonds et elle porte un jean, mais ne porte pas de pull orange. Ah, la voilà ! Elle parle avec un grand garçon de 18 ou 19 ans, aux cheveux bruns et frisés …*

**5**

Euh … Pardon, mais … est-ce que tu t'appelles Chloé ?

**6**

Oui, je suis Chloé. Et toi, tu es Nick, n'est-ce pas ?

Oui, c'est moi. Bonjour, Chloé.

Nick, je te présente mon frère, Hugo.

**7**

Ah, le frère de ma correspondante australienne. Bonjour, Nick.

**Dix minutes plus tard …**

Il est deux heures et quart. Rita est en retard, comme d'habitude !

Est-ce que vous attendez quelqu'un ?

Oui, nous attendons ma copine, Rita. Elle est toujours en retard.

Alors moi, j'en ai marre ! J'y vais. Ciao vous deux !

**8**

Salut !

Du calme, Chloé ! Tu vas me présenter ton copain ?

Rita ! Tu es impossible ! Ça fait une éternité qu'on attend !

Désolée. Rita, je te présente Nick. Nick, je te présente ma copine, Rita.

**9**

*Dans la rue Saint-Jean …*

Allons au cybercafé – il est moins cher que le café là-bas.

Oui, et on vend des pâtisseries délicieuses !

*Au cybercafé …*

Tu ressembles à ta sœur, Nick ?

Non, pas du tout. Suzanne est plus petite que moi et elle est blonde aux yeux bleus, comme ma mère. Je ressemble à mon père.

Moi aussi, je ressemble à mon père. Mais je ne suis pas aussi grande que papa, et je suis plus mince. Et je ne suis pas chauve !

Qu'est-ce que tu fais, Rita ?

Tu vas participer à un échange scolaire ?

J'espère que oui. Non, il n'y a pas de réponse.

Je vérifie si j'ai des e-mails. J'attends une réponse des Échanges Scolaires.

Patience ! Envoyons un e-mail à la sœur de Nick, en Australie.

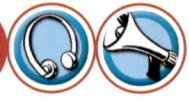

# Acting out the story

Use the next page to help you fully understand the cartoon story. Then, with some classmates, practise imitating the voices on the CD until you're ready to perform all or part of the story for the class.

# Points de prononciation

## Cognates

English and French words that look similar and have a similar meaning are called 'cognates'. Cognates are very helpful in understanding written French, but you must remember that the words are not pronounced the same way in both languages. You already know that certain letters and letter groups are pronounced differently in French. But there is also a difference in syllable emphasis.

In English, we emphasise some syllables more heavily than others, and not always in the same place in the word. Knowing which syllable to emphasise is hard for someone learning English. Think about how the stress changes when you say 'ph<u>o</u>tograph', 'phot<u>o</u>graphy' and 'photogr<u>a</u>phic'.

French speakers, by contrast, give fairly equal emphasis to all syllables, with the final syllable usually carrying a little more weight.

Try saying the English version of these cognates, noting where the stress falls in each word:

| | |
|---|---|
| **méthode** | **cathédrale** |
| **athlétisme** | **qualification** |
| **adorable** | **question** |
| **animal** | **salade** |
| **thermomètre** | **mathémathiques** |

Now, with your teacher, try pronouncing them in French. Remember what you've learned about the French pronunciation of **th** (t), **qu** (k) and **a** (ah), and try to give equal weight to each syllable.

# Vocabulaire

Together with your teacher, practise pronouncing the new vocabulary before doing the word detective activity in your *Workbook*.

| Noms | Adjectifs | Verbes | Mots et expressions utiles |
|---|---|---|---|
| le/la correspondant(e) | blond(e) | attendre | assez |
| le cybercafé | mi-long(ue) | correspondre | pas du tout |
| le copain | frisé(e) | vendre | quelqu'un |
| la copine | chauve | répondre | plus … que |
| la patience | raide | présenter | moins … que |
| la porte | mince | participer à | aussi … que |
| la réponse | impossible | envoyer | comme d'habitude |
| l'échange (*m*) scolaire | | se rencontrer | vérifier si on a des e-mails |
| l'e-mail (*m*) | | ressembler à | Du calme ! |
| les cheveux (*mpl*) | | | Ça fait une éternité qu'on attend ! |
| les yeux (*mpl*) | | | J'espère que oui ! |
| | | | J'y vais ! |

CYBAR-CAFE.com
INTERNET
JEUX RESEAUX
OUVERT
24 HEURES
369 DE L'ÉGLISE
522-0523

# En un mot

When you can confidently pronounce the new words on this page and you know what they mean, practise saying them with a classmate. Substitute the words in bold with choices from each box. Remember to make the feminine agreements if you are female, and use your imagination when saying who people look like.

> Ça te va bien, la barbe !

> Oui ! Je ressemble à notre prof d'histoire !

## être

petit(e) et mince    grand(e) et gros(se)    petit(e) et gros(se)    grand(e) et mince    de taille moyenne

**A**   Je suis **petit(e)** et **gros(se)** comme notre prof d'histoire !

**B**   Moi, je suis plus **gros(se)** que toi !

## avoir

 une moustache      une barbe

 un bouc      des lunettes

**A**   Regarde ! J'ai une **barbe** !

**B**   Ça alors ! Ça te va bien, **la barbe** !

## avoir les yeux

 bleus      verts

  gris      marron

**A**   Tu aimes les yeux **bleus** ?

**B**   Je préfère avoir les yeux **verts**.

## avoir les cheveux

blonds et frisés    roux et ondulés    noirs, longs et raides    blancs en brosse    châtains et mi-longs    bruns et courts

**A**   Regarde ! J'ai les cheveux **roux et ondulés** !

**B**   Ça alors ! Tu ressembles à **Nicole Kidman** !

## Verbalisez !

### Regular –re verbs

You can already use the large group of regular verbs known as **–er** verbs. There is another, smaller group of regular verbs with infinitives ending in **–re**: it includes the verbs **attendre** (to wait for), **correspondre** (to correspond), **vendre** (to sell) and **répondre** (to answer). Look at these regular **–re** verb conjugations and compare the endings with those of the regular **–er** verb. How many are different?

With both **–re** and **–er** verbs, the only endings pronounced are **–ons** and **–ez**.

| jouer – to play | attendre – to wait for | vendre – to sell |
|---|---|---|
| je joue**e** | j'attend**s** | je vend**s** |
| tu jou**es** | tu attend**s** | tu vend**s** |
| il/elle/on jou**e** | il/elle/on attend | il/elle/on vend |
| nous jou**ons** | nous attend**ons** | nous vend**ons** |
| vous jou**ez** | vous attend**ez** | vous vend**ez** |
| ils/elles jou**ent** | ils/elles attend**ent** | ils/elles vend**ent** |

As a class, practise reading through these **–re** verbs aloud. Then try conjugating the verb **répondre** (to answer). You'll find a more extensive list of regular **–re** verbs on page 50 of this *Coursebook*.

# Un chant aux cuillères musicales

In the 19th century, many **québécois** fur traders and wood-cutters ate their meals using a hand-crafted spoon which they carved from maple wood. At their evening camps, they would sing traditional songs from France, beating out the rhythm by 'playing the spoons'. Today, **les cuillères musicales** are still played and are popular as souvenirs. Try reciting your –re verb conjugations to the rhythm of the spoons!

*Moi, je vends ces cuillères musicales dans un magasin de souvenirs à Québec.*

*Moi, j'attends mon ami,*
*Tu attends tes grands-parents,*
*Il attend sa tatie,*
*Elle attend ses enfants,*
*Nous attendons nos cousins,*
*Vous attendez vos cousines,*
*Ils attendent leurs copains,*
*Elles attendent leurs copines.*

## Points de langue

### 1 The present tense

French people can find learning English hard because the English language has three different present tenses while French has only one.
For example, all these English sentences are in the present tense:

{ I wear jeans.
{ I am wearing jeans.
{ I do wear jeans.

{ She tidies her room.
{ She is tidying her room.
{ She does tidy her room.

But in French, they would all be expressed the same way:

**Je porte un jean.**          **Elle range sa chambre.**

Look again at the verbs **jouer**, **attendre** and **vendre** on the previous page. Can you give three English translations for each conjugation?

### 2 Making comparisons

To make comparisons between people or things in French, you use the expressions:

**plus … que** (more … than)
**moins … que** (less … than / not as … as)
**aussi … que** (as … as)

The words are placed either side of the adjective, just as they are in English. For example:

**Mon chien est <u>plus féroce que</u> son chien.**
My dog is <u>more fierce (fiercer) than</u> his dog.

**Elle est <u>moins patiente que</u> son frère.**
She's <u>less patient than (not as patient as)</u> her brother.

**La voile est <u>aussi dangereuse que</u> l'équitation.**
Sailing is <u>as dangerous as</u> horse-riding.

Remember that the adjective must agree with what it is describing.

How would you say this?
'Eva is taller than Anne.
Eva is not as tall as Léa.'

### 3 Using à in descriptions

Suzanne est blonde aux yeux bleus.

In descriptions, **à** used with a definite article can mean 'with'. For example:

**C'est l'homme <u>à la</u> barbe blanche.**
It's the man <u>with the</u> white beard.

**C'est le professeur <u>au</u> bouc.**
It's the teacher <u>with the</u> goatee.

**C'est la fille <u>aux</u> yeux bleus.**
It's the girl <u>with the</u> blue eyes.

Notice that **à** changes to **au** before a singular masculine noun, and to **aux** before a plural noun. These are the same changes you make with other expressions that use **à**.

# Dialogue

With a partner, use this dialogue to practise what you've learned. Use the choices to make your conversation different each time. When you can say your part confidently, change roles.

**B is trying to pick out A's friend from a class photo …**

**A** Voilà une photo de ma classe. Alors, où est | mon copain ?
ma copine ?

**B** Euh … | il
elle | est comment ? Est-ce qu' | il
elle | a les cheveux | raides ou frisés ?
raides ou ondulés ?

**A** Il
Elle | a les cheveux | roux
blonds
noirs | et | raides.
ondulés. | Et les yeux | verts.
bleus.
gris.

**B** Voyons … est-ce que c'est | ce garçon
cette fille | aux cheveux | mi-longs ?
longs ?

**A** Non. | Mon copain
Ma copine | a les cheveux courts et | il
elle | est moins | gros
grosse | que ça.

**B** D'accord …
Alors …
Ben … | il
elle | est plus mince que | ce garçon
cette fille | et | il
elle | a les yeux | verts.
bleus.
gris.

**A** Oui, mais | il
elle | porte des lunettes.

**B** Alors, c'est facile ! | C'est | ce garçon,
cette fille, | n'est-ce pas ? | Il
Elle | est | beau !
belle !

## Connexion culturelle

Although Australia and Canada are in opposite hemispheres, they have much in common. Both are sparsely populated, with vast expanses of inhospitable land – Australia has its inland deserts and Canada has its freezing, windswept Arctic regions.

Quebec is Canada's largest province. It is three times larger than France and, like France, is a place of great variety. Its historic cities and cosy inns contrast with the wild, natural beauty of its mountains, lakes and fiords. Like Australia, where most people live on the eastern coast, 80% of Quebec's population lives in urban centres along the giant St Lawrence River. Montreal is the largest of these with a population of 3.4 million, but the historic heart and capital of Quebec province is the smaller city of Quebec.

# Une histoire intéressante

**1** At the time of European exploration, the region along the St Lawrence River was occupied by the ancestors of Quebec's Native Canadians. In 1534, when French explorer Jacques Cartier landed there, the site of Quebec city was an Iroquois Indian village. In 1608 another French explorer, Samuel de Champlain, arrived at the same site to develop fur trade with the Indians. He founded the settlement which became known as Quebec (an Indian word for 'where the river narrows'). It soon became the centre of '**la Nouvelle France**' – the first French colony in North America.

**2** However, throughout the rest of the 17th century, British forces made repeated attacks attempting to take over Quebec. Finally, in 1759, the British defeated the French at Quebec in a battle that killed both the British and the French leaders. This famous battle was a turning point in Canada's history. In 1763 the Treaty of Paris gave all of Canada to Britain and large numbers of British people settled in what became Upper Canada (Ontario). Most of the French, however, stayed in Lower Canada (Quebec) where they maintained their own distinctive culture.

**3** Over the next two centuries, under a British government, the French Canadians fought to preserve rights to their own language, religion and education system. Within Quebec province today there remains a strong movement for separation from the rest of Canada. The people of Quebec think of themselves firstly as **Québécois(es)**, and secondly as Canadians. The white lily on the blue background is Quebec's official emblem and the provincial flag can be seen everywhere in Quebec, flying proudly beside Canada's maple leaf flag.

### Les Amérindiens

Native Canadians, also called First Nations and **Amérindiens**, have been in Quebec for more than 11 000 years. There are eleven groups including the Cree, Mohawk, Innu, Huron-Wendat, and the Innuit (once called Eskimos).

As in Australia and New Zealand, these indigenous peoples suffered with the arrival of Europeans. The number of Native Canadians dropped dramatically due to new diseases, the loss of land and food supplies, and the destruction of their traditional way of life.

Today, Native Canadians make up just a small percentage of the province's population. Most live on government reserves. Many Native Canadians are becoming more active in tracing their history and revitalising their traditional cultures, languages and spiritual beliefs.

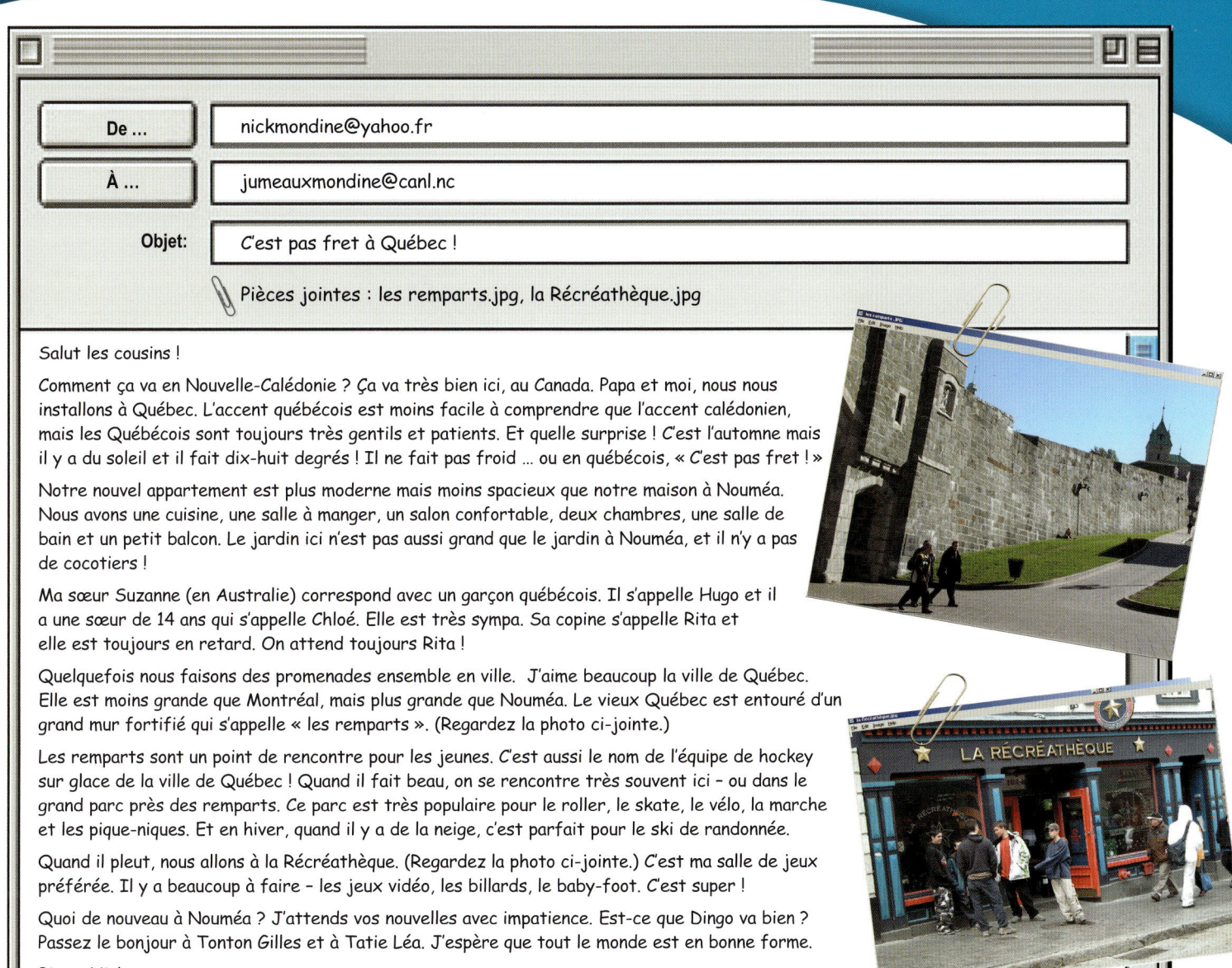

**De ...** nickmondine@yahoo.fr

**À ...** jumeauxmondine@canl.nc

**Objet:** C'est pas fret à Québec !

Pièces jointes : les remparts.jpg, la Récréathèque.jpg

Salut les cousins !

Comment ça va en Nouvelle-Calédonie ? Ça va très bien ici, au Canada. Papa et moi, nous nous installons à Québec. L'accent québécois est moins facile à comprendre que l'accent calédonien, mais les Québécois sont toujours très gentils et patients. Et quelle surprise ! C'est l'automne mais il y a du soleil et il fait dix-huit degrés ! Il ne fait pas froid … ou en québécois, « C'est pas fret ! »

Notre nouvel appartement est plus moderne mais moins spacieux que notre maison à Nouméa. Nous avons une cuisine, une salle à manger, un salon confortable, deux chambres, une salle de bain et un petit balcon. Le jardin ici n'est pas aussi grand que le jardin à Nouméa, et il n'y a pas de cocotiers !

Ma sœur Suzanne (en Australie) correspond avec un garçon québécois. Il s'appelle Hugo et il a une sœur de 14 ans qui s'appelle Chloé. Elle est très sympa. Sa copine s'appelle Rita et elle est toujours en retard. On attend toujours Rita !

Quelquefois nous faisons des promenades ensemble en ville. J'aime beaucoup la ville de Québec. Elle est moins grande que Montréal, mais plus grande que Nouméa. Le vieux Québec est entouré d'un grand mur fortifié qui s'appelle « les remparts ». (Regardez la photo ci-jointe.)

Les remparts sont un point de rencontre pour les jeunes. C'est aussi le nom de l'équipe de hockey sur glace de la ville de Québec ! Quand il fait beau, on se rencontre très souvent ici – ou dans le grand parc près des remparts. Ce parc est très populaire pour le roller, le skate, le vélo, la marche et les pique-niques. Et en hiver, quand il y a de la neige, c'est parfait pour le ski de randonnée.

Quand il pleut, nous allons à la Récréathèque. (Regardez la photo ci-jointe.) C'est ma salle de jeux préférée. Il y a beaucoup à faire – les jeux vidéo, les billards, le baby-foot. C'est super !

Quoi de nouveau à Nouméa ? J'attends vos nouvelles avec impatience. Est-ce que Dingo va bien ? Passez le bonjour à Tonton Gilles et à Tatie Léa. J'espère que tout le monde est en bonne forme.

Bises, Nick.

# Le français québécois

In 1969, the whole of Canada became officially bilingual. This is why even though most Canadians are English-speaking, you find English and French on product packaging, maps, road signs and tourist brochures all over Canada. Quebec is the only province with a majority of French speakers. Here, 94% of the population has French ancestry and French is the official language. It is also the dominant language, except in the city of Montreal where most people are bilingual.

Quebec has its own distinctive form of French called **québécois**. To people from France, the **québécois** accent and some expressions seem odd, just as Australian or New Zealand English may seem strange to people from England.

# Dictionnaire québécois

| français | québécois |
|---|---|
| la voiture | le char |
| l'essence | le gaz |
| Il fait froid ! | C'est fret ! Il fait frette ! |
| C'est nul ! | C'est plate ! |
| J'ai les cheveux en brosse. | J'ai une tête à kiwi. |

# Unité 1

## Jeu de rôle

With a classmate, create your own role-play, using the French you've already learned. Here's a suggestion:

You're chatting with a new friend whose family you've not yet met. You are discussing what different family members look like and who resembles whom.

You could:

- ask what members of each other's family look like
- describe hair/eyes/build of different members of your family
- discuss who resembles whom
- make some comparisons between family members using **plus/moins/aussi … que**

> Il est comment, ton père ?

> Il est petit, gros et chauve. Je suis plus beau que papa !

## À faire

### Clique Chic

Make a poster advertising the hair salon **Clique Chic**. Illustrate or use magazine pictures of a client (male or female), showing and describing their hair before (**avant**) and after (**après**) their visit to the salon.

**Cheveux fatigués ?**
*Nous avons la solution à Clique Chic !*

*avant* — *après*

Yannick, aux cheveux bruns, raides et longs

Yannick, aux cheveux blonds en brosse

### Têtes célèbres

Cut out a picture of a famous person and glue it on a page under the heading **Tête célèbre**. Underneath the photo, write four or five sentences describing the person's appearance (eyes, hair and build) and something to suggest why they are famous. You may also like to say how old they are, their nationality and what you think of them. When you've finished, you could have a game of **Qui est-ce ?** by reading out your descriptions to the class (without showing the photo) to see who can be first to guess the identity of **la tête célèbre**.

Elle adore la musique.
Elle a les cheveux bruns et longs.
Elle est mince.
Elle est canadienne.

# En ville

**Unité 2**

À CE SIGNAL
**TRAVERSEZ**

SI VOUS ÊTES DANS LA RUE
**CONTINUEZ**

SINON, PRESSEZ LE BOUTON ET
**ATTENDEZ**
LE SIGNAL

clignotant

PRESSEZ LE BOUTON ET
**ATTENDEZ**
LE SIGNAL

RENSEIGNEMENTS:
691-6000

VILLE DE québec

**PIÉTONS**

**ATTENDEZ**
LE SIGNAL

## Learn how to:

- Ask how to get to places
- Ask if something is nearby
- Identify some places in town
- Give directions to some places in town
- Say where something is
- Give instructions
- Say you don't understand
- Ask for something to be repeated

## Learn about:

- Landmarks in French and québécois **towns**
- French and québécois **shops**

## Il y a une pharmacie près d'ici ?

*Nick et Chloé vont passer l'après-midi dans le Vieux Québec …*

Après le match, attendez devant le stade ! D'accord ?

Oui, d'accord. À bientôt, Hugo !

Bonne chance pour le match !

Ben … nous sommes ici, à la Porte Saint-Louis.

Alors, pour aller au Château Frontenac, c'est loin ?

Non, c'est tout près. Nous prenons cette rue et c'est tout droit.

*Dix minutes plus tard …*

Voilà le château devant nous ! Et à gauche, c'est le Saint-Laurent.

Ça alors ! Ne bouge pas ! Je vais prendre une photo.

Et la statue à droite, c'est Samuel de Champlain ?

Oui, c'est ça. Et là-bas, à côté du musée, c'est l'office du tourisme. Tu veux un plan de la ville ?

Oui. Bonne idée !

Zut ! Il est déjà cinq heures ! Nous prenons le bus à cinq heures trente !

Oui, mais je veux aller à la pharmacie pour maman !

*Deux heures plus tard …*

Du calme ! On a encore trente minutes.

Ce n'est pas loin. On tourne à droite, puis on traverse la rue …

Attends Chloé ! Attends ! Le feu est rouge ! Zut !

VROUM !
VROUM !

*À 5h10, Nick cherche Chloé …*

Pardon, mais … est-ce qu'il y a une pharmacie près d'ici ?

Euh … oui. Va tout droit, puis tourne à droite après l'hôtel de ville, et il y a une pharmacie en face du dep.

En face du dep ? Je ne comprends pas.

**À 5h15 ...**

Oui, descendez cet escalier, prenez la première rue à gauche, et continuez tout droit. Il y a une pharmacie derrière l'église.

Mais madame, vous parlez trop vite ! Vous voulez répéter, s'il vous plaît ?

**À 5h20 ...**

Euh, excusez-moi monsieur. Est-ce qu'il y a une pharmacie près d'ici ?

Euh ... voyons. Tournez à gauche, et encore à gauche après les magasins, puis remontez la première rue à droite. Il y a une pharmacie en face de l'hôpital.

Merci beaucoup, monsieur.

**À 5h25 ...**

Nick !

Chloé !

Et ben ... alors, grosse maligne, tu vas toujours trop vite !

Et toi, gros malin, vraiment tu planes ! Alors, vite ! Nous sommes en retard !

**À 6h05 au stade de hockey sur glace ...**

Allez tout droit, puis tournez à gauche devant les toilettes, descendez l'escalier et voilà !

Regarde, Nick ! Le numéro 22, c'est Hugo !

Allez les Remparts !

## Acting out the story

Use the next page to help you fully understand the cartoon story. Then, with some classmates, practise imitating the voices on the CD until you're ready to perform all or part of the story for the class.

# Points de prononciation

Remember to emphasise syllables more evenly than you do in English.

Many cognates have letter combinations that make nasal sounds in French. Remember that nasal sounds are made when a vowel is followed by **n** or **m**. There are four different nasal sounds:

## on/om

Say 'on' without letting your tongue touch the roof of your mouth, lips slightly pursed. Try these cognates:

**c**on**fortable**   **c**on**cert**   **f**on**ction**   **m**on**stre**
**n**om**bre**   **c**om**pagn**on   **c**om**pétiti**on

## an/am, en/em

Make a sound similar to on/om, but with your jaw dropped open. Try these cognates:

**s**an**dwich**   **s**an**dale**   **grand-parent**
**d**e**scente**   **c**on**tent**   **t**em**pérature**
**n**ov**embre**   **d**éc**embre**

## un/um

Say 'un' without letting your tongue touch the roof of your mouth. Now try these cognates:

**j**un**gle**   **p**un**k**   **b**un**galow**   **h**um**ble**

## in/im, yn/ym, ain/aim

This time say 'an' without letting your tongue touch the roof of your mouth. Try these cognates:

**lat**in   **int**elligent   **in**formation
**sim**ple   **im**possible   **im**patient
**syn**thétique   **sym**bole   **sym**phonie
**terr**ain   **tr**ain

# Vocabulaire

Together with your teacher, practise pronouncing the new vocabulary before doing the word detective activity in your *Workbook*.

### Noms

le stade
le château
le magasin
le musée
le plan de la ville
le bus
le feu
la place
la statue
la pharmacie
l'hôpital (*m*)
l'escalier (*m*)
l'église (*f*)
l'office (*m*) du tourisme

### Verbes

bouger
continuer
tourner
traverser
répéter
remonter
descendre
prendre
comprendre

### Directions

derrière
devant
en face (de)
à côté (de)
tout près (de)
loin (de)
à gauche (de)
à droite (de)
tout droit

### Mots et expressions utiles

Bonne chance !
Gros malin !
  Grosse maligne !
Tu planes !
pour aller à …
c'est ça
excusez-moi
encore

CENTRE COMMUNAUTAIRE

BIBLIOTHÈQUE

MAIRIE

### En un mot

# PLAN DU VIEUX QUÉBEC

## LÉGENDE

1. la gare
2. la gare des autobus
3. le marché
4. l'hôpital (m)
5. la salle de jeux
6. le théâtre
7. l'hôtel (m) de ville
8. le poste de police
9. la cathédrale
10. le restaurant
11. l'hôtel (m)
12. la place
13. le château
14. la poste
15. le musée
16. l'église (f)
17. le port
18. la citadelle
19. le parc
? l'office (m) du tourisme

When you can confidently pronounce the new words on this page and you know what they mean, practise them with a classmate.

**A**, the tourist, substitutes the words in bold with different places on the map.

**B**, a tourist office employee, locates the place by giving the grid references.

Remember to use the correct articles and to change roles.

**A** Pardon, madame/monsieur. Où est **la poste**, s'il vous plaît ?

**B** **La poste ?** C'est ici, à **D4**.

## Verbalisez !

### Prendre – to take

Although the infinitive **prendre** ends in **–re**, it is *not* a regular **–re** verb. Compare it with the regular **–re** verb **vendre**. Can you spot the differences?

| vendre – to sell | prendre – to take |
|---|---|
| je vend**s** | je prend**s** |
| tu vend**s** | tu prend**s** |
| il/elle/on vend | il/elle/on prend |
| nous vend**ons** | nous pren**ons** |
| vous vend**ez** | vous pren**ez** |
| ils/elles vend**ent** | ils/elles prenn**ent** |

As a class, practise reading **prendre** aloud until you are confident with the pronunciation. As with other irregular verbs, you will need to learn it by heart.

Try conjugating **comprendre** (to understand) and **apprendre** (to learn). They work the same way as **prendre**.

Can you give three English translations for each conjugation?

---

## CHANT DE LA TRIBU

A good way to learn a verb by heart is to turn the verb into a tribal chant. On the left-hand side of the board, write all parts of the verb **prendre**, and on the other side, write some class suggestions for different ways to complete the sentences. **Le chef** (your teacher or a volunteer) leads the tribal chant starting with the two parts of the sentence at the top of the list. **La tribu** (the class) joins in and, when all are chanting in unison, **le chef** indicates a change to either half of the sentence by pointing to a new variation. When this is being chanted in unison, another change is indicated, and so on. Add some more endings to these and have a go!

| je prends | mon caleçon |
|---|---|
| tu prends | le petit train |
| il prend | un sac |
| elle prend | ce gros melon |
| on prend | la deuxième rue à gauche |
| nous prenons | • |
| vous prenez | • |
| ils prennent | • |
| elles prennent | |

# Points de langue

## 1 Giving orders & instructions

When you drop the 'you' from a verb to give an order or instruction, you are using the *imperative* form of the verb. Because there are two French words for 'you' – **tu** and **vous** – there is an imperative form for each.

For the polite/plural form, just use the part of the verb that goes with **vous**, but without the **vous**. For example:

**Vous écoutez.**

**Écoutez !**

For the familiar form, use the part of the verb that goes with **tu**, but without the **tu**. For example:

**Tu prends cette rue-ci.**

**Prends cette rue-ci.**

**BUT** Verbs that end in **–es** in their **tu** form (including all **–er** verbs) drop the **–s** from the **tu** part of the verb. For example:

**Tu continues tout droit.**   **Tu tournes à gauche.**

**Continue tout droit.**   **Tourne à gauche.**

**Aller** also drops the **–s** from the **tu** part of the verb. For example:

**Tu vas tout droit.**

**Va tout droit.**

To give a negative instruction, just use **ne ... pas** either side of the verb in the usual way. For example:

**Ne bouge pas !**
Don't move!

How many examples of the imperative can you find in the story on pages 14–16?

Classroom orders like **Écoutez !** end in **–ez** because the teacher is using the plural imperative to speak to a group.

## 2 Prepositions

Words that indicate where something is in relation to something else are called *prepositions*. For example:

**Le chien est *sous* la maison.**
The dog is *under* the house.

Here are some prepositions you already know:

| | |
|---|---|
| **dans** | in |
| **sous** | under |
| **sur** | on |
| **devant** | in front (of) |
| **derrière** | behind |

Some French prepositions require the word **de** if there is a noun following. For example:

**La poste est loin.**

**BUT**   **La poste est loin *de* la gare.**

These prepositions all require *de* before a noun:

| | |
|---|---|
| **près (de)** | near |
| **loin (de)** | far (from) |
| **à côté (de)** | beside |
| **en face (de)** | opposite, facing |
| **à gauche (de)** | to the left (of) |
| **à droite (de)** | to the right (of) |

When you use a preposition followed by **de**, you need to make changes to **de** if the noun following is masculine or plural.

| Type of noun | Example |
|---|---|
| masc. sing. | Le café est près **du** cinéma. |
| fem. sing. | Le café est près **de la** poste. |
| sing. starting with vowel or mute 'h' | Le café est près **de l'**église. |
| | Le café est près **de l'**hôtel. |
| plural | Le café est près **des** magasins. |

## 3 Asking for directions

There are a number of different ways you can ask for directions.

If you are looking for something that there's probably *more than one of*, you can say, for example:

**Il y a un hôtel près d'ici ?**

If you are looking for a place that there's probably *only one of*, you can ask, for example:

**La gare, s'il vous plaît ?** or

**Où est la gare, s'il vous plaît ?** or

**Pour aller à la gare, s'il vous plaît ?**

When you use **Pour aller à ...** before a masculine or plural noun, you need to make the same changes as you do for other expressions that use **à**.

| Type of noun | Example |
|---|---|
| masc. sing. | Pour aller **au** château ? |
| fem. sing. | Pour aller **à la** banque ? |
| sing. starting with vowel or mute 'h' | Pour aller **à l'**office du tourisme ? Pour aller **à l'**hôpital ? |
| plural | Pour aller **aux** magasins ? |

## Dialogue

With a partner, use these dialogues to practise what you've learned. Make your conversation different each time. When you can say your part confidently, change roles.

**A tourist stops a passer-by for directions …**

**A** | Pardon, Excusez-moi, | monsieur. madame. | Pour aller | à la gare, au marché, | s'il vous plaît ?

**B** | Descendez Prenez | cette rue, et tournez à | droite gauche | après | la poste. l'église. | C'est | tout droit. en face.

**A** | Bon, Alors, | je | descends prends | cette rue, puis je tourne à | droite gauche | après | la poste. l'église.

**B** | Voilà ! Bravo !

**A** | Est-ce qu'il y a | une banque un cybercafé | près | de la gare ? du marché ?

**B** | Oui. Traversez | la place le parc | en face à côté | de la gare. du marché. | Puis prenez la | première deuxième | rue à | gauche. droite.

**A** | Mais | je ne comprends pas, vous parlez trop vite, | monsieur ! madame ! | Vous voulez répéter, s'il vous plaît ?

## Connexion culturelle

**Le Vieux Québec** is the historic heart of the larger city of **Québec** and is surrounded by fortified walls (**les remparts**). The narrow winding streets inside the walls are typical of the old parts of many historic French towns.

Old town centres in France and Quebec are often a maze of one-way streets because the roads are too narrow for today's vehicles to pass. Parking can be almost impossible!

These towns have a very different feel from the younger, more open towns of Australia and New Zealand where there is often no real centre to the town. By contrast, in France and Quebec, signs pointing to **Centre Ville** are seen in every town, large or small.

Follow these signs and you are likely to find yourself at **la place** – the town square – such as **la place des Cocotiers** in Noumea, or **la place du Huit Septembre** in Besançon. An important feature of French towns, **la place** serves as a meeting place for the locals and is often the site of **le marché** – the weekly market.

In these old town centres, you still find some of the small, specialist shops – **les petits commerces** – that thrived before the arrival of supermarkets. The big stores, known as **les grandes surfaces** are usually in the suburbs where parking is easier.

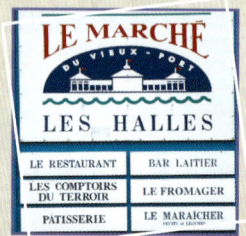

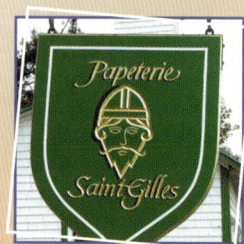

## Les petits commerces

| | |
|---|---|
| la boucherie | la boulangerie |
| l'épicerie | la charcuterie |
| la crémerie | la fromagerie |
| la librairie | la papeterie |
| la pâtisserie | la pharmacie |
| la poissonnerie | la quincaillerie |

Avec l'arrivée des grandes surfaces, beaucoup de ces magasins spécialisés perdent leurs clients.

## Les grandes surfaces

« Les grandes surfaces » sont des grands magasins en libre service qui offrent un vaste choix de produits. Les grands magasins (avec une surface de plus de 2.500m$^2$) s'appellent « les hypermarchés ». D'habitude les grandes surfaces sont à l'extérieur des villes.

## Les marchés

Les marchés vendent des produits frais : légumes, fruits, fleurs, viandes, poissons, œufs et fromages. Toutes les villes françaises ont un marché en plein air une ou deux fois par semaine. Certaines villes ont des marchés permanents et couverts.

# DANS LA RUE

## OÙ PRÉFÉREZ-VOUS FAIRE LES COURSES ?

### Estelle, 26 ans, et Arnaud, 25 ans

**Est-ce que vous préférez faire vos courses dans les petits commerces ou dans les grandes surfaces ?**

D'habitude, nous aimons faire du shopping dans les hypermarchés. Il y a plus de choix et les produits ne sont pas aussi chers que dans les petits commerces.

**Vous achetez tout à l'hypermarché – même les produits frais ?**

Non. Pour les fruits et les légumes, c'est moins cher et plus frais au marché. Nous allons toujours au marché le dimanche matin. C'est amusant !

### Marie-France, 75 ans

**Vous faites vos courses dans les grandes surfaces, madame, ou dans les petits commerces ?**

Moi, je préfère les petits commerces. Ils sont plus chers que les supermarchés, mais ils sont plus personnalisés.

**Vous allez toujours chez les petits commerçants ?**

Je vais très rarement dans les supermarchés, parce que je perds trop de temps à chercher les produits. C'est trop fatigant à mon âge !

### Christian, 1 an et Élodie, 31 ans

**Vous faites toujours les courses dans les supermarchés ?**

Normalement oui, parce que les supermarchés sont très pratiques. Tout est là dans un seul magasin – crémerie, boucherie, épicerie, charcuterie …

**Vous n'allez pas quelquefois dans les petits commerces ?**

Pas souvent. Mais je préfère acheter le poisson à la poissonnerie. C'est plus frais.

### Manuel, 56 ans, propriétaire d'une épicerie traditionnelle

**Est-ce que les petits commerces perdent leurs clients ?**

Ce n'est pas facile aujourd'hui, parce que les jeunes préfèrent les grandes surfaces. La majorité de mes clients ont 60 ans et plus. Ils achètent rarement des provisions pour la semaine – ils préfèrent acheter une ou deux choses tous les jours. Les personnes âgées aiment les petits commerces parce qu'ils aiment parler aux commerçants. C'est sympa comme ça !

## Dictionnaire québécois

| québécois | français |
|---|---|
| magasiner | faire du shopping, faire les courses |
| le cégep | le lycée |
| le dépanneur (le dep) | une épicerie souvent ouverte 24h/24h |
| la tabagie | le (bureau de) tabac |
| le poste de police | le commissariat/la gendarmerie |

## Jeu de rôle

With a classmate, create your own role-play, using the French you've already learned. **Student A** is visiting **l'office du tourisme** to get a town map and directions to different places in town. **Student B** works at the tourist office and is very efficient, but rather impatient when **A** is a bit slow to catch on. Or you may have other ideas to make your characters interesting.

Make sure you:
- greet each other
- ask if a town map is available
- use different ways of asking for directions to a variety of places
- give directions using a variety of verbs in the imperative form of **vous**
- say thank you and goodbye

You could also:
- suggest an itinerary for a walk around town
- say you don't understand
- ask for something to be repeated

> Où est la poste, s'il vous plaît ?

> La poste ? Prenez cette rue puis …

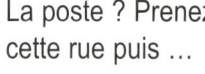

## À faire

### Plan de la ville

Design a new **plan de la ville** that will become part of a tourist brochure for a francophone town. Label the streets and a minimum of ten landmarks. You could also do an enlargement of the town's **centre ville**, showing the various shops and services. Number and identify the features in a legend **(une légende)**. **Le plan du Vieux Québec** on page 18 will give you some ideas.

### Tour de la ville

Use your **plan de la ville** to prepare a tour route for a company conducting bus tours of your francophone town. Use arrows to mark in the tour route on your map. The route should take you past the town's main attractions. Then write a commentary for the tour guide, directing the tourists' attention to these features. The prepositions on page 20 will give you some ideas. You could also practise saying the commentary and make an audio recording that can be used when the guide is not available for the tour.

> … et voilà la cathédrale Saint-Joseph à gauche. En face de la cathédrale, il y a une statue de Jean Martin …

# Au café

Faubourg St-Jean-Baptiste ▸

Vieux-Québec / Haute-Ville ▸

## Learn how to:

- Take someone's order for food and drink
- Say what you're having to eat and drink
- Talk about what you would like
- Agree and disagree with an opinion
- Specify what flavour/filling you want
- Say what never happens
- Use –ir verbs

## Learn about:

- **Some** québécois **specialities**
- **Halloween in** Québec
- **Dog sledding**

## Qu'est-ce que vous prenez ?

*C'est le 31 octobre. Nick et Chloé sculptent une citrouille pour Halloween …*

Qu'est-ce que tu vas porter ce soir, Nick ?

Pour Halloween ? Je ne sais pas.

Moi, je vais porter un costume de sorcière.

Ah bon ? Voici Rita ! Elle semble très contente aujourd'hui.

Salut, mes amis ! Devinez ! Je vais participer à un échange en France !

C'est super ! Bravo, Rita !

Ça alors ! Il faut fêter ça ! Allons au café ensemble !

*Quinze minutes plus tard, au centre ville …*

Vous voulez prendre une poutine chez Ashton ?

Qu'est-ce que c'est, une poutine ?

C'est une spécialité québécoise … et c'est dégoûtant !

Je ne suis pas d'accord ! C'est délicieux !

*Finalement, ils décident de manger à La Belle Gaufre …*

Bonjour, les jeunes ! Qu'est-ce que vous voulez ?

Euh … je voudrais une gaufre végétarienne. J'ai faim, moi !

Moi aussi ! Je voudrais une gaufre aux asperges, s'il vous plaît.

Nick et Chloé félicitent Rita …

Dix minutes plus tard …

*Plus tard, ils parlent de leurs costumes d'Halloween …*

**Chez Rita …**

## Acting out the story

Use the next page to help you fully understand the cartoon story. Then, with some classmates, practise imitating the voices on the CD until you're ready to perform all or part of the story for the class.

# Points de prononciation

## Cognates with –ble

There are many cognates that end in the letters –**ble**. In French, these letters make the sound 'bl', unlike in English where they are pronounced like the word 'bull'. In French there is always a slight extra emphasis on the syllable before the –**ble**. Try saying these:

horri**ble**      adora**ble**      ta**ble**
ensem**ble**      capa**ble**      miséra**ble**
terri**ble**      possi**ble**

## Cognates with i/y or oi/oy

To say the following cognates correctly in French you need to take care with pronouncing the letters **i** or **y** ('ee') and **oi** or **oy** ('wah'). Remember **h** is always silent.

arr<u>i</u>ve       d<u>i</u>alogue      sc<u>i</u>ence
s<u>i</u>lence      cl<u>i</u>ent        surpr<u>i</u>se
host<u>i</u>le      hist<u>oi</u>re      t<u>oi</u>lettes
r<u>oy</u>al        f<u>oy</u>er

Tu es horrible !

Mais non !
Je suis adorable !

# Vocabulaire

Together with your teacher, practise pronouncing the new vocabulary before doing the word detective activity in your *Workbook*.

| Noms | Verbes | Adjectifs | Mots et expressions utiles |
|---|---|---|---|
| le café (au lait) | choisir | dégoûtant(e) | |
| le bonbon | finir | frais, fraîche | |
| le sirop d'érable | remplir | végétarien(ne) | |
| la gaufre | rougir | vrai(e) | je voudrais |
| la taxe | décider | | encore |
| l'addition (f) | féliciter | | être d'accord |
| l'erreur (f) | fêter | | Moi non plus. |
| les asperges (f) | oublier | | Félicitations ! |
| le costume | sembler | | Et avec ça ? |
| le fantôme | sculpter | | Avec plaisir ! |
| le drap | | | Devinez ! |
| la sorcière | | | finalement |
| la citrouille | | | Hip hip hip hourra ! |

## En un mot

When you can confidently pronounce the new words on this page and know what they mean, use these activities to practise them with a classmate. Substitute the words in bold with appropriate items. Be careful to use the correct articles and remember to change roles.

A customer is complaining to the waiter that some essential items are missing from his table setting.

(A) Monsieur, je n'ai pas **de couteau** !

(B) Vous voulez **un couteau**, monsieur ?

un verre

la carte

une assiette

une serviette (de table)

un couteau

une tasse

une cuillère

une fourchette

## MENU MIDI

*Faire une pause & savourer un instant de détente au Café des Théâtres*

**Nos sandwichs**
Sandwich* au jambon . . . . . . . . . . .2,85 €
Sandwich* au fromage . . . . . . . . .3,05 €
Sandwich* aux tomates . . . . . . . .2,50 €
Sandwich* à la salade de poulet . .2,95 €
Sandwich* au saumon fumé . . . . . .3,00 €
Croissant au jambon-fromage . . . .3,65 €
Croissant au poulet . . . . . . . . . . .3,65 €

*Sandwich: choix de baguette ou pain complet*

**Nos desserts**
Glace à la vanille . . . . . . . . . . . . .2,50 €
Glace au chocolat . . . . . . . . . . . . .2,50 €
Glace à la fraise . . . . . . . . . . . . . .2,50 €
Tarte au sucre . . . . . . . . . . . . . . .2,50 €
Tarte aux pommes . . . . . . . . . . . .2,50 €
Tarte aux poires . . . . . . . . . . . . . .2,50 €

Note that **sandwich** and **croissant** are both masculine. **Glace** and **tarte** are both feminine.

The waiter is taking a customer's order.

(A) Qu'est-ce que vous prenez comme sandwich ?

(B) Je prends **un sandwich au fromage**.

(A) Et comme dessert, qu'est-ce que vous voulez ?

(B) Comme dessert, je voudrais **une tarte aux pommes**.

# Verbalisez !

## Regular –ir verbs

You can now use two different types of regular verbs: –**er** and –**re**. A third group of regular verbs with infinitives ending in –**ir** includes the verbs **finir** (to finish), **rougir** (to blush), **choisir** (to choose) and **remplir** (to fill).

Look at the endings of these regular –**ir** verbs and compare them with the regular –**er** and –**re** verb endings. Are there any similarities?

Can you give three English translations for each conjugation?

| parler – to speak | vendre – to sell | finir – to finish | choisir – to choose |
| --- | --- | --- | --- |
| je parle | je vends | je finis | je choisis |
| tu parles | tu vends | tu finis | tu choisis |
| il/elle/on parle | il/elle/on vend | il/elle/on finit | il/elle/on choisit |
| nous parlons | nous vendons | nous finissons | nous choisissons |
| vous parlez | vous vendez | vous finissez | vous choisissez |
| ils/elles parlent | ils/elles vendent | ils/elles finissent | ils/elles choisissent |

Practise saying all these verbs through with your teacher, noticing which endings are pronounced and which are silent. Learn the three sets of regular verb endings by heart – it's a short cut to being able to use hundreds of verbs.

# CHANT DE LA TRIBU

As a class, decide which of the –**ir** verbs from the list above could be easily added to and used to create your own **chant de la tribu**. On the left-hand side of the board, write all parts of the verb, and on the other side suggestions for different ways to complete the sentences. Start with the two parts of the sentence at the top of each list. **Le chef** leads the tribal chant and indicates a change to either half of the sentence only when **la tribu** (the class) is chanting in unison.

je finis
tu finis
il finit
•
•
•
•
•

mon déjeuner
tes devoirs
la glace au chocolat
•
•
•
•

# Unité 3

## Points de langue

### 1 Another use for prendre

The verb **prendre** is used (and not **avoir**) when talking about what food or drink people are having. For example:

– **Qu'est-ce que vous prenez, jeune homme ?**

– **Je prends une gaufre au sirop d'érable, s'il vous plaît.**

### 2 Saying 'I would like …'

You already use **je veux** to say what you want. A more polite way to say this is **je voudrais …** meaning 'I would like …'. Both are parts of the same, very useful verb, **vouloir** – to wish or to want.

You can put a *noun* after using **vouloir** to say *what* you would like. For example:

– **Tu veux une gaufre ?**

– **Non, je voudrais/veux un sandwich.**

Or you can put an *infinitive* after using **vouloir** to say what you would like *to do*. For example:

– **Je voudrais/veux manger une gaufre.**

– **Et moi, je voudrais/veux prendre un sandwich.**

You will learn more of the verb **vouloir** later.

### 3 Foods, flavours & fillings

In French, to say what filling or flavour a food has, or to say what it is served with, you need to use the word **à**. For example:

| | |
|---|---|
| **une glace à la vanille** | – a vanilla icecream |
| **une gaufre au sirop d'érable** | – a maple syrup waffle |
| **une tarte aux pommes** | – an apple tart |

Notice that before a singular masculine noun, **à** changes to **au**. Before a plural noun, **à** changes to **aux**. These are the same changes you made in **Unité 1** when using **à** to mean 'with' in descriptions.

### 4 Never

You know how to use the words **ne … pas** either side of the verb to say what is *not* happening. For example:

**Je ne rougis pas !**    I'm not blushing!

You can do the same thing with **ne … jamais** to say what *never* happens. For example:

**Je ne rougis jamais !**    I never blush!

If you are using the partitive article after **ne … jamais**, you do the same thing as after **ne … pas**. Just use **de** instead of **de la**, **de l'**, **du** or **des**. For example:

Du café, mademoiselle ?

Non, merci. Je ne prends jamais **de** café.

### 5 Agreeing & disagreeing

You already use **moi aussi** to agree with someone making an affirmative statement. To agree with someone making a negative statement, you use **moi non plus**. For example:

| | |
|---|---|
| **Je prends un café.** | **Moi aussi.** |
| I'm having a coffee. | Me too. |
| **Je ne prends jamais de café.** | **Moi non plus.** |
| I never have coffee. | Me neither. |

With appropriate changes to the verb, you can use the expression **être d'accord** to talk about agreeing and disagreeing. For example:

| | |
|---|---|
| **Je suis d'accord.** | I agree. |
| **Vous êtes d'accord ?** | Do you agree? |
| **Nous ne sommes pas d'accord.** | We don't agree. |

# Dialogue

With a partner, use this dialogue to practise what you've learned. Use the choices to make your conversation different each time. When you can say your part confidently, change roles.

**A is a waiter/waitress in a café. B is the customer …**

**A** | Bonjour, Bonsoir, | mademoiselle. monsieur. madame. | Qu'est-ce que vous | prenez ? voulez ? désirez ?

**B** | Je | voudrais prends | un croissant une salade | s'il vous plaît. | J'adore | les croissants. les salades.

**A** | Bon … D'accord … | un croissant. une salade. | Et comme boisson ? Et avec ça ? | Du café ? Du thé ?

**B** | Non, je ne prends jamais de | café. thé. | Vous avez Il y a | du jus de tomates ? du jus de pommes ?

**A** | Bien sûr, Mais oui, | mademoiselle. monsieur. madame. | Et après ? Qu'est-ce que vous | prenez désirez voulez | comme | dessert ? fromage ?

**B** | Merci, mais je ne prends jamais de | dessert. fromage.

**A** | Vraiment ? Ah bon ? | C'est tout, alors ?

**B** | Oui, c'est tout. | C'est Ça fait | combien, | monsieur ? madame ?

**A** | Voilà l'addition. | Ça fait | six euros quarante-cinq, quatre euros soixante, cinq euros quatre-vingts, | mademoiselle. monsieur. madame.

LES PANINIS

LES SANDWICHES

| | SEUL | AVEC SALADE |
|---|---|---|
| | 3⁹⁵ | 5³⁰ |
| | 3⁹⁵ | 5³⁰ |

| | SEUL | AVEC SALADE |
|---|---|---|
| Jambon | 3⁹⁵ | 5³⁰ |
| Jambon fromage | 4⁹⁵ | 6³⁰ |
| (Brie, cheddar ou gruyère) | | |
| Dinde fumée et | 5⁹⁵ | 7³⁰ |
| ...terie | 4⁹⁵ | 6³⁰ |
| ...n, mortadelle et salami) | | |

César classique ... 5⁹⁵ ... 7⁹⁵
...poulet grillé ... 5⁹⁵ ... 7⁹⁵
Brie ...

Légumes ...

Jambon et ...

## LES QUICHES ET LES TOURTES

| | SEUL | AVEC SALADE |
|---|---|---|
| Lorraine | 4²⁵ | 5⁶⁰ |
| Poulet poireaux | 4⁴⁵ | 5⁸⁰ |
| Scandinave | 5⁹⁵ | 7³⁰ |
| (Saumon fumé, asperges, épinards) | | |

## LES FRITES

| | PETITE | GRANDE |
|---|---|---|
| Frites | 1⁷⁵ | 2²⁵ |
| Frites sauce | | 2²⁵ |
| Poutine | | 3⁹⁵ |

## LES DESSERTS

| | |
|---|---|
| Tarte du jour | 2⁷⁵ |
| Gâteau du jour | 2⁵⁰ |
| Muffin maison | 1³⁵ |
| Carré aux framboises | 2⁵⁰ |
| Biscuit | 1²⁵ |

## Connexion culturelle

La Poutine, fraîche sept jours sur sept, depuis 32 ans!
Frites fraîches coupées à la main, sauce maison, fromage en grains frais!

### La poutine

**La poutine** is a **québécois** speciality available across the province in all sorts of eating places – classy restaurants, cheap cafés and fast-food places like Ashtons and McDonalds. Have a look at this tray cover from Ashtons and work out exactly what's in **une poutine**.

As you can see, it's not exactly healthy food. But love it or hate it, it's warm and filling when the temperature drops to –25°C!

La Poutine, fraîche sept jours sur sept, depuis 32 ans!
Frites fraîches coupées à la main, sauce maison, fromage en grains frais!

### Le sirop d'érable

It was the Native Canadians who first taught Europeans how to make Canada's famous maple syrup. In early spring, the sap rises in the sugar maple trees and nowadays it is sucked out through tubes which snake through the maple forest to a nearby **cabane à sucre** (sugar shack). Here it is cooked in cauldrons until it is transformed into the sweet maple syrup. Quebec produces 75% of the world's maple syrup.

### Halloween

Halloween originates from an ancient festival that marked the eve of the Celtic new year – a time when ghosts, demons and witches were believed to be active. It has long been an important celebration in North America, and is increasingly popular in France.

In Quebec on the evening of 31 October, most adults are ready at their doors with bags of lollies – **des sacs à bonbons** – for the arrival of young people in weird disguises or fancy dress, who threaten to play a trick if they don't receive a treat.

Shops and supermarkets are stocked with Halloween supplies and decorations for the entire month beforehand. Throughout October, many supermarkets have specially printed bags, with advice to young people for when they go out to 'trick or treat'. What precautions are suggested on this one?

Laisse tes parents inspecter tes bonbons avant de les manger.
Ne mange pas de bonbons qui ne sont pas enveloppés.
Fais ta tournée seulement dans un voisinage que tu connais bien.
Porte un costume de couleur claire visible dans le noir.
Ne porte ni vêtements ni masques inflammables.
Marche sur les trottoirs et traverse les rues seulement aux intersections.
Ne passe pas entre les voitures stationnées.
Ne fais pas ta tournée seul(e).
Sonne aux portes en groupe et attends toujours à l'extérieur des maisons

*Text from actual supermarket bag.*

## Dictionnaire québécois

| français | québécois |
|---|---|
| le petit-déjeuner | le déjeuner |
| le déjeuner | le dîner |
| le dîner | le souper |
| la boisson | le breuvage |
| le sandwich (baguette) | le sous-marin |
| le pain grillé, le toast | la rôtie |

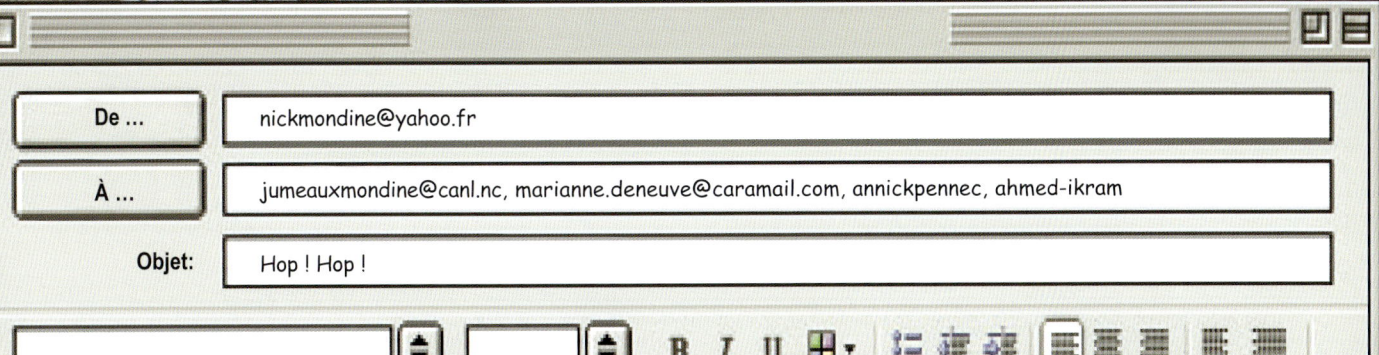

**De ...** nickmondine@yahoo.fr

**À ...** jumeauxmondine@canl.nc, marianne.deneuve@caramail.com, annickpennec, ahmed-ikram

**Objet:** Hop ! Hop !

Salut tout le monde ! Vous êtes en bonne forme ? Ici les premières neiges commencent. Le week-end, papa et moi avons visité un centre pour les chiens de traîneau. Quelle expérience ! 200 chiens et chiots – des huskies et des malamutes. Ils semblent vraiment féroces, mais en réalité, ils sont très affectueux.

Les huskies sont originaires de Sibérie et les malamutes d'Alaska. J'adore les malamutes. Ils sont énormes et vraiment magnifiques ! Les huskies sont moins grands et moins forts que les malamutes, mais ils sont plus rapides. Très souvent, les yeux des huskies sont de couleurs différentes – un œil bleu et l'autre, marron. C'est bizarre !

Dans une équipe de dix chiens, il y a normalement quatre malamutes et six huskies – et seulement une chienne, parce que les femelles se disputent ! D'habitude, on a deux chiens pour tirer une personne. Les mêmes chiens restent toujours ensemble dans la même équipe, et le chef de l'équipe – le leader – est le chien le plus intelligent. Il est très important parce qu'il guide les autres chiens. Les chiens travaillent seulement en hiver quand il y a de la neige. Ils ne travaillent pas en été parce qu'ils n'aiment pas la chaleur.

Les chiots commencent leur entraînement à l'âge de sept mois, mais ils ne portent pas de harnais avant d'être adulte. Chaque chien reconnaît son nom et la voix de son maître. Tous les chiens comprennent ces ordres :

**en avant** = allons-y !   **dji** = à droite   **yah** = à gauche   **hop ! hop !** = plus vite
**whoah !** = arrête   **dji maison** = demi-tour à droite   **yah maison** = demi-tour à gauche

C'est fascinant, n'est-ce pas ?

C'est le 30 octobre et demain on fête Halloween ici. Tous les magasins et les jardins sont décorés de sorcières, de fantômes et d'énormes citrouilles orange. Demain soir, les jeunes vont faire la tournée pour demander des bonbons aux voisins. C'est chouette !

Félix et Emma : Comment ça va sous les tropiques ? Est-ce que la saison des cyclones commence ?

Marianne, Annick et Ahmed : De grandes nouvelles ! En décembre, papa finit son travail à Québec, puis nous allons retourner à Besançon pour Noël ! Et vous allez rencontrer Rita, la copine québécoise de Chloé. Elle va venir en France avec nous, parce qu'elle va participer à un échange scolaire à Dijon.

J'attends vos nouvelles – écrivez-moi bientôt !

Bises, Nick

## Jeu de rôle

With one or two classmates, create your own role-play, using the French you've already learned.

**Student A** is a waiter/waitress at a café.
**Student B** is a customer who has come in for a meal.
**Student C** could accompany **Student B** as another customer.

Add extra interest by giving your characters some personality – impatient, cheerful, indecisive, etc.

**Student A** could:
- greet the customer(s)
- ask what the customer wants
- offer the menu
- say what is/isn't available
- ask what the customer wants to eat/drink
- agree or disagree
- ask if that's all

**Student B** (and **C**) could:
- greet the waiter/waitress
- say you're hungry/thirsty
- ask what's available
- ask for the menu
- say what you want
- say what you think of a menu item
- ask how much something is
- ask for the bill
- say something is/isn't expensive
- say there's a mistake

## À faire

### Votre café

Imagine you own a café in France or Quebec. Design a lunch menu, putting the items you offer under appropriate headings. You could include sandwiches, desserts and drinks. Use the menus on pages 30 and 33 to give you an idea of prices – Canadian dollars are used in Quebec, euros are used in France.

Make sure you invent a name for your café. Cafés in France and Quebec are often named after the street they are in, or after a famous person (like **Le Petit Champlain**), or after something they're near (like **le Café du Théâtre** or **le Café de la Poste**).

### Set de table

Design a paper placemat for a café table to keep customers occupied while they're waiting for their meals. Create one or more word puzzles – for example, **cache-cache** (word-find) or **mots croisés** (crossword) – using as many words as possible related to food, drink and dining. As many Canadians are bilingual, your clues could be in English.

# Bon voyage !

## Learn how to:

- Talk about travelling by bus/plane/train
- Say where you're going from and to
- Say what sort of ticket you want
- Ask what time the train leaves
- Ask which platform the train leaves from
- Ask for and say phone numbers
- Say what is necessary
- Use reflexive verbs
- Use French quotation marks

## Learn about:

- Canadian railways
- La SNCF
- Les TGV
- The Channel Tunnel and the Eurostar
- Accent variations between France and Quebec

# Unité 4

## Vos billets, s'il vous plaît !

*Aujourd'hui Nick et son père quittent le Québec pour retourner en France. Ils sont accompagnés de Rita qui participe à un échange à Dijon, près de Besançon.*

**Ils sont à l'aéroport de Montréal ...**

> Les passagers sur le vol Air Canada 870 – destination Paris – sont invités à se présenter à la porte numéro trois ...

> Allons, les enfants ! Il faut partir !

1

**Dans l'avion ...**

> Qu'est-ce que tu préfères, Rita ? La place côté fenêtre ou côté couloir ?

> Ça m'est égal. Zut ! J'ai trop de bagages !

> Hé ! Faites attention !

> Pardon, monsieur. Je suis désolée !

2

**Trente minutes plus tard, ils sont en route vers la France ...**

> Qu'est-ce que vous désirez ? Des biscuits ?

> Non merci. Je ne mange jamais de biscuits.

> Vous ne voulez pas de boisson, alors ?

> Si, je voudrais un coca, s'il vous plaît.

3

> Vous vous amusez bien, vous deux ?

> Oui, nous nous amusons très bien ... n'est-ce pas, Rita ?

> Oui, je m'amuse à écouter de la musique. C'est super !

4

**Quatre heures plus tard, Rita se réveille. Nick n'est pas là ...**

> Nick est aux toilettes.

> Je vais aller aux toilettes, moi aussi.

5

*Rita attend un peu, puis …*

Tu es là, Nick ? Vite ! Je suis pressée ! Qu'est-ce que tu fais ?

Je me lave ! Attends un peu !

*À l'aéroport Charles de Gaulle, deux heures plus tard : Rita, Nick et son père prennent le bus pour aller à la gare à Paris …*

Patience, mademoiselle !

Pardon, monsieur ! Je m'excuse …

Bravo, Rita ! Tu rougis encore !

Youpi ! Je suis en France ! Je suis à Paris ! Mais … tu ne sembles pas content, Nick.

Si, je suis content, mais je suis un peu fatigué. De Montréal à Paris en avion, de l'aéroport à la gare en bus, de la gare à Dijon en train … C'est fatigant !

Nick ! Rita ! Donnez vos bagages au conducteur, puis montez dans le bus !

*Ils arrivent à la gare de Lyon, trente minutes plus tard …*

Nick, va acheter nos billets, s'il te plaît. Deux billets pour Besançon, un pour Dijon. D'accord ?

D'accord. On se rencontre où ?

Devant la salle d'attente, dans vingt minutes. Il faut se dépêcher.

... et deux billets pour Besançon, s'il vous plaît.

*Nick achète les billets au guichet.*

Aller simple ou aller-retour ?

Aller simple, s'il vous plaît.

Voilà. Ça fait cent cinquante-deux euros.

Alors, le train part de quelle voie ?

De la voie numéro dix-neuf ... dans dix minutes ! Il faut changer à Dijon.

Allons-y ! N'oubliez pas de composter vos billets !

*Dans le train ...*

Vos billets, s'il vous plaît !

Où est mon billet ? Ah, le voilà.

*Ils continuent leur voyage vers Besançon ...*

*Deux heures plus tard, ils descendent à la gare de Dijon. Rita rencontre sa famille d'accueil et Nick et son père changent de train ...*

Attention au départ !

Nick ! Quel est ton numéro de téléphone ?

C'est le 03 81 87 92 90. N'oublie pas de téléphoner ! Au revoir, Rita !

Tu téléphones à Marianne ?

Oui ... Salut, Marianne ! C'est moi, Nick ! Je suis en France !

## Acting out the story

Use the next page to help you fully understand the cartoon story. Then, with some classmates, practise imitating the voices on the CD until you're ready to perform all or part of the story for the class.

## Points de prononciation

### Cognates with –eur

Many cognates related to occupations end in the letters **–eur**. These letters are pronounced like 'ur' in the English word 'fur'. Try saying these words correctly, remembering to give more weight to the last syllable and equal emphasis to the others.

**profess<u>eur</u>**   **doct<u>eur</u>**   **act<u>eur</u>**   **mass<u>eur</u>**
**dans<u>eur</u>**   **direct<u>eur</u>**   **inspect<u>eur</u>**

### Cognates with –er

In French, the letters **–er** are pronounced differently from the letters **–eur**.

At the end of an infinitive, **er** is pronounced like **é**. Try pronouncing these cognates correctly:

**arriv<u>er</u>**   **commenc<u>er</u>**   **dîn<u>er</u>**   **invit<u>er</u>**
**pronon<u>er</u>**   **répét<u>er</u>**   **visit<u>er</u>**

In most other situations, **–er** makes a similar sound to the English word 'air'. Try saying these cognates:

**sup<u>er</u>be**   **p<u>er</u>sonne**   **s<u>er</u>pent**   **c<u>er</u>tain**
**dess<u>er</u>t**   **s<u>er</u>viette**   **p<u>er</u>manent**

How would you say these infinitives? **terminer fermer**

## Vocabulaire

Together with your teacher, practise pronouncing the new vocabulary before doing the word detective activity in your *Workbook*.

### Noms

un aller simple
un aller-retour
l'aéroport (m)
l'avion (m)
le bagage
le billet
le biscuit
le conducteur
le départ
le guichet
le numéro de
  téléphone
le passager
le vol
la voie
la famille d'accueil
la place côté fenêtre
la place côté couloir
la salle d'attente

### Verbes

accompagner
changer
composter
donner
retourner
téléphoner
voyager
monter
descendre
partir
s'amuser
s'excuser
se laver
se dépêcher
se réveiller

### Mots et expressions utiles

Ça m'est égal.
être invité à se présenter à …
en avion/bus/train
être pressé(e)
de … à …
un peu
si

## En un mot

When you can confidently pronounce the French destinations on **le tableau des trains au départ** (departure board), practise asking for and giving departure information by working with a classmate. Substitute the words in bold with the appropriate departure times and platform numbers for the different destinations. When you are confident, remember to change roles.

**A** Le premier train pour **Marseille** part à quelle heure ?

**B** Voyons … le premier train pour **Marseille** part à **onze heures cinquante**.

**A** Il part de quelle voie ?

**B** Il part de la voie **B**.

When you understand and can confidently pronounce the highlighted words on the tickets, practise saying them with a classmate.

First read through the exchange below. Then role-play the conversation that took place to buy these tickets by substituting the words in bold with the appropriate details. Remember to change roles when you are confident.

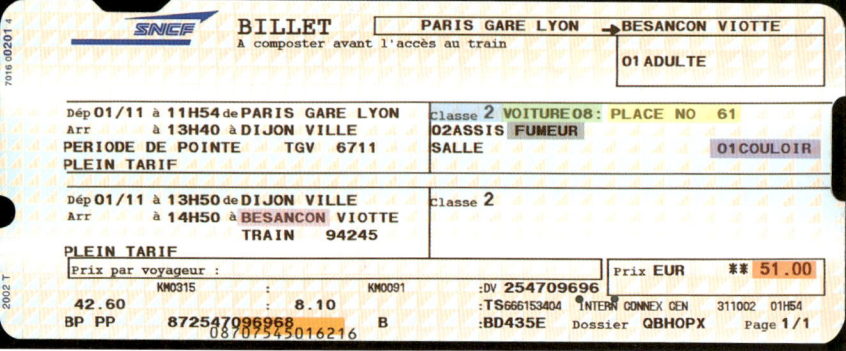

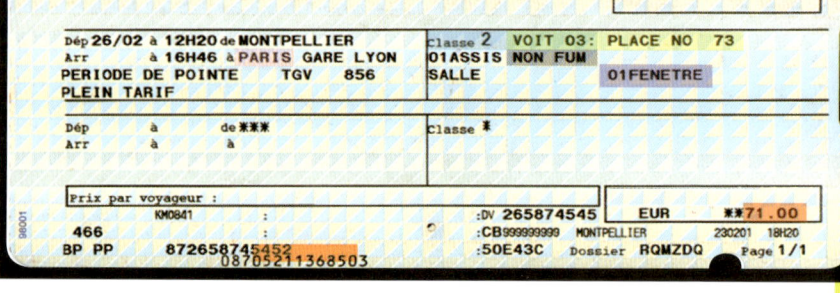

**A** Un aller simple pour **Lyon**, s'il vous plaît.

**B** Première classe ou deuxième classe ?

**A** **Première classe** s'il vous plaît, et **non-fumeur**.

**B** Place côté couloir ou côté fenêtre ?

**A** Côté **fenêtre**, s'il vous plaît.

**B** Voilà ! C'est **la voiture numéro seize** et la place **cinquante-cinq**. Ça fait **soixante-deux** euros.

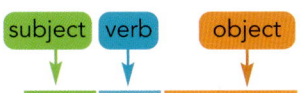

## Verbalisez !

## Reflexive verbs

Subject = doer of the action. Object = receiver of the action.

With most verbs, the action is done by the *subject* to an *object*. For example:

subject verb object

**Nick lave** *la voiture*.   Nick is washing *the car*.

Reflexive verbs are different because the action is done by the *subject* to the *subject*.
For example:

**Nick *se* lave.**   Nick is washing *himself*.

In other words, the action is reflected back. This is shown by an extra part called the reflexive pronoun. Reflexive pronouns can often be translated as 'myself', 'yourself', 'himself', etc.

Here are two fully conjugated reflexive verbs. Memorise the pattern of reflexive pronouns by saying the verbs aloud as a class.

| **se laver** – to wash (oneself), to have a wash | **s'amuser** – to enjoy oneself, to have fun |
|---|---|
| **je me lave** <br> I wash (myself) | **je m'amuse** <br> I enjoy myself |
| **tu te laves** <br> you wash (yourself) | **tu t'amuses** <br> you enjoy yourself |
| **il/elle/on se lave** <br> he/she/one washes (himself/herself/oneself) | **il/elle/on s'amuse** <br> he/she/one enjoys himself/herself/oneself |
| **nous nous lavons** <br> we wash (ourselves) | **nous nous amusons** <br> we enjoy ourselves |
| **vous vous lavez** <br> you wash (yourselves) | **vous vous amusez** <br> you enjoy yourselves |
| **ils/elles se lavent** <br> they wash (themselves) | **ils/elles s'amusent** <br> they enjoy themselves |

When the verb starts with a vowel or mute 'h', **me**, **te** and **se** change to **m'**, **t'** and **s'**.

## CHANT DE LA TRIBU

As a class, create **un chant de la tribu** using the reflexive verb **s'amuser**. Write the verb conjugations on the left of the board, and some class suggestions for different places where people enjoy themselves on the right. Take care to use the correct form of **à** before each noun. **Le chef** indicates a change to either half of the sentence, only when **la tribu** (the class) is chanting in unison.

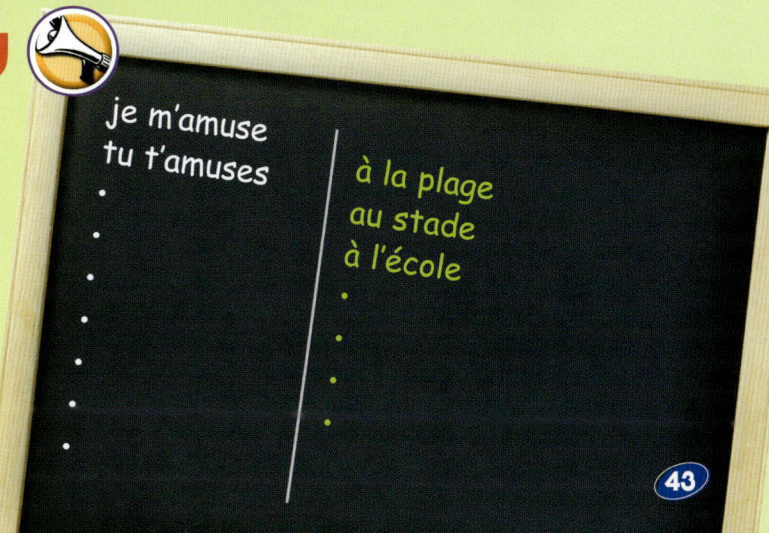

je m'amuse
tu t'amuses
.
.
.
.
.
.

à la plage
au stade
à l'école
.
.
.

## Points de langue

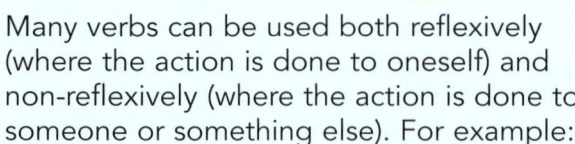

How many examples of reflexive verbs can you find in the cartoon story?

### 1 More about reflexive verbs

Although all reflexive verbs have the extra part called the reflexive pronoun, it is not always translated as 'myself', 'yourself', etc. This means that many verbs that are reflexive in French are not *obviously* reflexive in English. For example:

**s'appeler** – to be named (to call oneself)
**se dépêcher** – to hurry (oneself)

Many verbs can be used both reflexively (where the action is done to oneself) and non-reflexively (where the action is done to someone or something else). For example:

**Je me réveille à sept heures.**
I wake (myself) up at 7 o'clock.

**Je réveille ma sœur à sept heures trente.**
I wake my sister at 7.30.

### 2 Il faut … with infinitives

You already know certain verbs that can be used with infinitives, for example, to say what you like/hate/prefer/want or are going to do.

**Elle aime voyager.**
**Tu préfères prendre le train ?**

**Nous allons descendre à Dijon.**
**Je veux aller à Besançon.**

By using **il faut** (it is necessary) with an infinitive you can say what needs to, must, or has to be done. For example:

**Il faut partir !**
{
It is necessary to leave.
We/You need to leave.
We/You must leave.
We/You have to leave.
}

How many different ways can you translate this sentence?

**Il faut changer à Dijon.**

**Il faut** is the only present tense form of the irregular verb **falloir** – to be necessary.

### 3 Si

**Oui** is not the only way to say 'yes' in French. To answer 'yes' to a *negative* question, you use **si**. For example:

– Tu n'aimes pas voyager ?
– Si, j'adore voyager !

Tu ne sembles pas content, Nick.

Si, je suis content.

### 4 « Les guillemets »

French quotation marks are called **les guillemets** and they look like this: « … ». Use them in much the same way as you use English quotation marks. For example:

« Attends ! Tu vas trop vite ! » s'exclame Rita.
« Mais, vraiment, tu planes ! » répond Nick.

You will see more examples of these on page 47. In longer conversations, **les guillemets** are used only to show the start and finish of the conversation. Each change of speaker is indicated by a dash. For example:

« Attends ! Tu vas trop vite ! s'exclame Rita.
– Mais vraiment, tu planes ! répond Nick.
– Est-ce que nous sommes en retard ?
– Oui. Le train part à onze heures ! »

# Dialogue

With a partner, use this dialogue to practise what you've learned. Use the choices to make your conversation different each time. When you can say your part confidently, change roles.

**1** The scout leader is alerting scouts to an early start for tomorrow's excursion …

**A** | Tu te réveilles / Vous vous réveillez | à quelle heure, | d'habitude ? / le matin ?

**B** | Je me réveille / On se réveille / Nous nous réveillons | toujours / d'habitude | à sept heures. / à sept heures et quart. / à sept heures vingt.

**A** | Alors, demain il faut | se réveiller / arriver à la gare | très tôt. / à six heures et demie.

**2** The next morning at the SNCF ticket office …

**A** | Je m'excuse / Nous nous excusons | monsieur, / madame, | mais | je suis / nous sommes | en retard ! / pressé(e)(s) !

**B** | Qu'est-ce que vous | désirez, / voulez, | mademoiselle ? / jeune homme ?

**A** | Un / Deux | aller(s) simple(s) / aller(s)-retour(s) | pour | Paris, / Besançon, | s'il vous plaît.

**B** | Vous préférez quelle classe ? | Première ? / Deuxième ?

**A** | Première / Deuxième | classe, s'il vous plaît. | Mais vite, | monsieur ! / madame ! | Je suis / Nous sommes | pressé(e)(s) ! / en retard !

**B** | Bon … / D'accord … | Aller simple, / Aller-retour, | première / deuxième | classe, | fumeur, / non-fumeur, | pour | Paris. / Besançon.

**A** | Mais il faut se dépêcher | monsieur ! / madame ! | On va / Il faut | partir dans | cinq / sept | minutes !

**B** | Du calme, / Patience, | mademoiselle ! / jeune homme ! | Ça fait | cinquante-deux / cent quatre | euros. | Il faut changer à Dijon.

GUICHET

## Connexion culturelle

# Train travel in Canada and France

When the Canadian Pacific Railway was completed in 1885, the separate parts of Canada were linked for the first time. A string of luxury hotels – like the Château Frontenac in Quebec – were built from east to west, to encourage people to travel by rail.

But the vast, sparsely populated expanses of Canada, like Australia, mean that the rail networks don't reach all areas. So while Canadians are proud of their coast-to-coast railway, most find car travel more convenient.

France, by contrast, has a highly developed rail network and French people coming to Canada and Australia are often surprised to find that many smaller towns do not have a train service. In France, train travel is so fast, reliable and convenient that millions of people use trains daily rather than cars, avoiding the inconveniences of parking and traffic congestion. In fact, trains now compete with planes as a mode of rapid travel within France and Europe.

To find a railway station in France, look for the sign **SNCF**.

To find a railway station in Canada, look for the sign **VIA Rail**.

## La SNCF

The French rail system, known as the SNCF – **la Société Nationale des Chemins de Fer Français** – has a worldwide reputation for speed and punctuality. The vast railway network radiates out from Paris to all parts of France.

In Paris, there is not one main train station, but six, each one servicing a different area of France. For example, **la Gare du Nord** services the north of France, **la Gare de l'Est**, the east, **la Gare de Lyon**, the south and south-east.

With the SNCF carrying more than 800 million passengers a year, these huge stations are a bustle of activity – and a favourite place for pickpockets! To cope with the huge numbers of people, there are both ticket windows (**les guichets**) and automatic ticketing machines (**les billeteries automatiques**). You need to validate (**composter**) your ticket before you board the train, or you could pay a hefty fine.

## Le TGV et l'Eurostar

**Le TGV** (pronounced té-gé-vé) stands for **le Train à Grande Vitesse**. France has led the world in the development of high-speed trains since the 1950s, and is rivalled only by Japan for its quality and speed of service. Since France built its first high-speed line between Paris and Lyon in 1981, and set the world speed record of 515.3 km/h in 1990, the TGV services have extended to more French cities as well as to neighbouring countries.

Les lignes TGV

The TGV Eurostar enables passengers to travel at 300 km/h in luxury between Paris, Brussels and London. When the Channel Tunnel opened in 1994, it became the first dry land link between England and France since the Ice Age. It consists of three interconnected, parallel tunnels – two for trains travelling in opposite directions and one for maintenance access – all 45 metres under the seabed. This sleek international train speeds silently across northern France, passes under the English Channel, and emerges again in the English countryside to complete its journey to London just three hours later.

Les billeteries automatiques acceptent les cartes de crédit.

Il faut composter votre billet avant de monter dans le train.

## Chapitre 2

# Danger
*dans le*
## Canadien

Enfin, le taxi arrive. L'inspecteur Jacques Tremblay se dépêche. Son train part dans quinze minutes. Les queues devant les guichets sont plus longues que d'habitude. Il lui faut acheter son billet à la billeterie automatique. Mince ! Il déteste les machines !

Dix minutes plus tard, il composte son billet à l'entrée de la voie numéro deux. Il regarde tout droit. Le voilà ! *Le Canadien* – un train d'une élégance classique ! Tremblay adore voyager en train. C'est plus romantique et moins fatigant que la voiture. Mais aujourd'hui, il voyage pour le travail, pas pour le plaisir.

Il regarde encore la description du suspect. En fait, c'est une suspecte – une femme entre trente et quarante ans, grande, mince et belle. Elle a les cheveux noirs, raides et mi-longs et les yeux bleus. Elle porte un pullover jaune, un pantalon gris et un blouson noir – et elle est dans ce train.

« Attention au départ ! » annonce le haut-parleur.

Tremblay monte dans le train et cherche sa place côté fenêtre. Bon ! La place d'à côté n'est pas occupée.

❈ ❈ ❈

Le contrôleur arrive.

« Vos billets, s'il vous plaît ! »

Tremblay donne son billet au contrôleur et se présente. Il explique sa mission, puis il accompagne le contrôleur pour commencer ses recherches.

Ils entrent dans une voiture de première classe. Tremblay regarde attentivement à gauche ... puis à droite. Il y a une femme côté couloir qui regarde nerveusement le contrôleur. Soudain, elle se lève, se retourne et marche vers les toilettes.

# À la gare de Québec

## Vous êtes français(e) ou québécois(e) ?

Listen to the man from Paris and the woman from Quebec reading these sentences. What differences do you notice in their pronunciation? What do you notice about the way that French and **québécois** people say their phone numbers?

**« Deux allers-retours, s'il vous plaît. »**

**« Il y a cinq cents voyageurs dans le train. »**

**« Où est le contrôleur ? »**

**« Je prends mon dîner chez moi. »**

**« Son numéro de téléphone, c'est le 42 56 01 79. »**

## Jeu de rôle

Using the French that you have already learned, create your own role-play: one of you is the traveller, the other is the ticket clerk. The traveller arrives at the station with little time to buy a ticket and doesn't know where things are. Try to include some more problems for the traveller to overcome before they catch the train. Use at least one reflexive verb (for example **s'excuser**, **se dépêcher**) and both tonal and **est-ce que** type questions.

You could include questions/comments about:
- destination
- type of ticket/seat
- how much it costs
- where parts of the station are
- which platform the train leaves from
- what time the train leaves
- whether it is necessary to change trains

## À faire

### La famille Rigolo

**La famille Rigolo** has fun, no matter where they are! Create your own **famille Rigolo** and make a few pages for their family photo album.

Cut out magazine pictures of people (or use some photos of your own family or friends) showing the various family members enjoying themselves in different places. You will need 6–8 pictures, one for each of the singular pronouns (**je**, **tu**, **il/elle**) and one for each of the plural pronouns (**nous**, **vous**, **ils/elles**).

For each picture, write a caption or speech bubble saying where the different family members enjoy themselves. Use an appropriate part of the reflexive verb **s'amuser** and be sure to use the correct form of **à** before the place.

Nous nous amusons à la maison.

Voici Estelle. Elle s'amuse au cybercafé.

### Jeu de l'oie – En ville

Make a French board game about a day exploring a French or **québécois** town. On a large blank sheet, create a route of about thirty squares numbered from 1–30. The route should start and finish at the same square – **la gare SNCF/VIA**. Some of the squares should feature places in town (see **Unité 2** for ideas), some should give instructions directing players to these places, and some should be blank except for their number.

To direct players to skip forward, use either **Allez à …** or **Il faut aller à …** .

To send players back, use either **Retournez à …** or **Il faut retourner à …** .

For 'miss a turn', use either **Passez un tour** or **Il faut passer un tour**.

Look at this example to get some ideas. When your board is finished, have a game with some friends using dice and markers. The first to finish, wins.

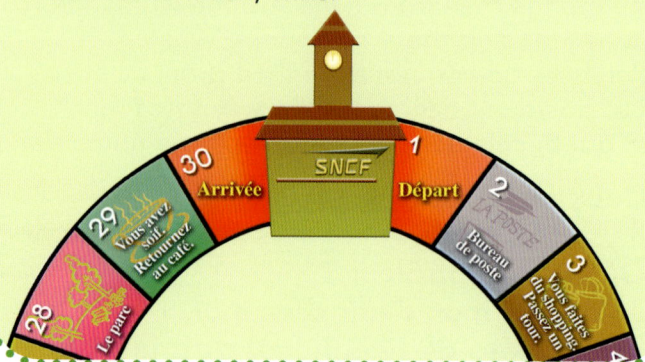

## Nombres cardinaux

| | | | | | |
|---|---|---|---|---|---|
| 0 | zéro | 16 | seize | 78 | soixante-dix-huit |
| 1 | un | 17 | dix-sept | 79 | soixante-dix-neuf |
| 2 | deux | 18 | dix-huit | 80 | quatre-vingts |
| 3 | trois | 19 | dix-neuf | 81 | quatre-vingt-un |
| 4 | quatre | 20 | vingt | 82 | quatre-vingt-deux |
| 5 | cinq | 21 | vingt et un | 90 | quatre-vingt-dix |
| 6 | six | 22 | vingt-deux | 91 | quatre-vingt-onze |
| 7 | sept | 23 | vingt-trois | 92 | quatre-vingt-douze |
| 8 | huit | 30 | trente | 99 | quatre-vingt-dix-neuf |
| 9 | neuf | 40 | quarante | 100 | cent |
| 10 | dix | 50 | cinquante | 101 | cent un |
| 11 | onze | 60 | soixante | 102 | cent deux |
| 12 | douze | 70 | soixante-dix | 200 | deux cents |
| 13 | treize | 71 | soixante et onze | 201 | deux cent un |
| 14 | quatorze | 72 | soixante-douze | 300 | trois cents |
| 15 | quinze | 73 | soixante-treize | 999 | neuf cent quatre-vingt-dix-neuf |
| | | 74 | soixante-quatorze | 1.000 | mille |
| | | 75 | soixante-quinze | 2.000 | deux mille |
| | | 76 | soixante-seize | 1.000.000 | un million |
| | | 77 | soixante-dix-sept | 2.000.000 | deux millions |

## Nombres ordinaux

premier, première
deuxième
troisième
quatrième
cinquième
sixième
septième
huitième
neuvième
dixième
onzième
douzième

## Jours de la semaine

lundi
mardi
mercredi
jeudi
vendredi
samedi
dimanche

## Mois de l'année

| | |
|---|---|
| janvier | juillet |
| février | août |
| mars | septembre |
| avril | octobre |
| mai | novembre |
| juin | décembre |

## Saisons

le printemps
l'été *(m)*
l'automne *(m)*
l'hiver *(m)*

## Couleurs

jaune
rose
rouge

bleu(e)
brun(e) – hair, etc.
gris(e)
noir(e)
vert(e)

blanc(he)
violet(te)
bleu marine *(inv)*
marron *(inv)* – eyes, clothes, etc.
orange *(inv)*

Remember that the French present tense can be translated in three ways. For example: **je porte** = I wear/I am wearing/I do wear

To conjugate regular verbs, drop the infinitive ending (**–er**, **–re** or **–ir**) and add the appropriate ending to the remaining stem, as shown.

## Regular –er verbs

| **port**er – to wear, to carry (infinitive) | |
|---|---|
| je port**e**<br>I wear | nous port**ons**<br>we wear |
| tu port**es**<br>you wear | vous port**ez**<br>you wear |
| il/elle/on port**e**<br>he/she/one wears | ils/elles port**ent**<br>they wear |

Other common **–er** verbs:
**demander** – to ask
**écouter** – to listen (to)
**fermer** – to close
**oublier** – to forget
**parler** – to speak
**quitter** – to leave
**terminer** – to finish

## Regular –re verbs

| **vend**re – to sell (infinitive) | |
|---|---|
| je vend**s**<br>I sell | nous vend**ons**<br>we sell |
| tu vend**s**<br>you sell | vous vend**ez**<br>you sell |
| il/elle/on vend<br>he/she/one sells | ils/elles vend**ent**<br>they sell |

Other common **–re** verbs:
**attendre** – to wait (for)
**correspondre** – to correspond
**descendre** – to go down
**entendre** – to hear
**perdre** – to lose
**rendre** – to give back, return
**répondre** – to answer, reply

## Regular –ir verbs

| **fin**ir – to finish (infinitive) | |
|---|---|
| je fin**is**<br>I finish | nous fin**issons**<br>we finish |
| tu fin**is**<br>you finish | vous fin**issez**<br>you finish |
| il/elle/on fin**it**<br>he/she/one finishes | ils/elles fin**issent**<br>they finish |

Other common **–ir** verbs:
**blanchir** – to go/turn white
**choisir** – to choose
**grandir** – to grow
**grossir** – to get fatter
**maigrir** – to get thinner
**punir** – to punish
**réfléchir** – to reflect, think
**remplir** – to fill
**réussir** – to succeed
**rougir** – to blush

## Reflexive verbs

| **se lav**er – to wash oneself (infinitive) | |
|---|---|
| je **me** lav**e**<br>I wash (myself) | nous **nous** lav**ons**<br>we wash (ourselves) |
| tu **te** lav**es**<br>you wash (yourself) | vous **vous** lav**ez**<br>you wash (yourselves) |
| il/elle/on **se** lav**e**<br>he/she/one washes<br>him/her/oneself | ils/elles **se** lav**ent**<br>they wash (themselves) |

Other common reflexive verbs:
**s'amuser** – to enjoy (oneself), have fun
**s'appeler** – to be named, called
**se disputer** – to argue
**s'ennuyer** – to be bored
**s'excuser** – to excuse oneself, be sorry
**s'habiller** – to dress (oneself)
**s'installer** – to settle in
**se passer** – to happen
**se presser** – to hurry (oneself)
**se réveiller** – to wake (oneself)

# Semi-regular verbs

## manger – to eat (infinitive)

| | |
|---|---|
| je mange<br>I eat | nous mangeons<br>we eat |
| tu manges<br>you eat | vous mangez<br>you eat |
| il/elle/on mange<br>he/she/one eats | ils/elles mangent<br>they eat |

Remember that **–er** verbs ending in **–cer** and **–ger** have irregularities in the **nous** form. For example:

commencer – nous commençons
prononcer – nous prononçons
changer – nous changeons
manger – nous mangeons
ranger – nous rangeons
voyager – nous voyageons

Other semi-regular **–er** verbs make changes to the stem when the ending is silent (all forms except **nous** and **vous**). Verbs ending in:

**–yer** change the **y** to **i**, for example:
**pay**er – **vous payez** but **tu paies**
**envoy**er – **vous envoyez** but **tu envoies**

**–é_er** change the **é** to **è**, for example:
**esp**é**rer** – **vous espérez** but **tu espères**
**préf**é**rer** – **vous préférez** but **tu préfères**

**–e_er** change the **e** to **è**, for example:
**ach**e**ter** – **vous achetez** but **tu achètes**
OR
double the consonant, for example:
**s'appel**er – **vous vous appelez** but
**tu t'appelles**

# Irregular verbs

## avoir – to have (infinitive)

| | |
|---|---|
| j'ai<br>I have | nous avons<br>we have |
| tu as<br>you have | vous avez<br>you have |
| il/elle/on a<br>he/she/one has | ils/elles ont<br>they have |

## aller – to go (infinitive)

| | |
|---|---|
| je vais<br>I go | nous allons<br>we go |
| tu vas<br>you go | vous allez<br>you go |
| il/elle/on va<br>he/she/one goes | ils/elles vont<br>they go |

## être – to be (infinitive)

| | |
|---|---|
| je suis<br>I am | nous sommes<br>we are |
| tu es<br>you are | vous êtes<br>you are |
| il/elle/on est<br>he/she/one is | ils/elles sont<br>they are |

## faire – to do, to make (infinitive)

| | |
|---|---|
| je fais<br>I do/make | nous faisons<br>we do/make |
| tu fais<br>you do/make | vous faites<br>you do/make |
| il/elle/on fait<br>he/she/one does/makes | ils/elles font<br>they do/make |

## prendre – to take (infinitive)

| | |
|---|---|
| je prends<br>I take | nous prenons<br>we take |
| tu prends<br>you take | vous prenez<br>you take |
| il/elle/on prend<br>he/she/one takes | ils/elles prennent<br>they take |

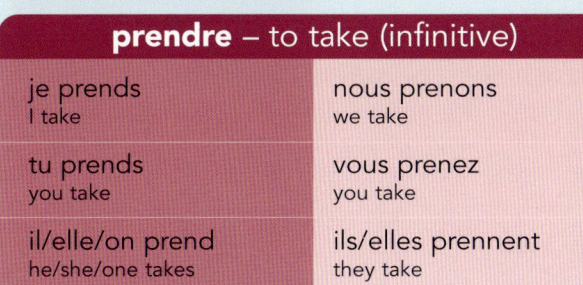

The verbs **comprendre** (to understand) and **apprendre** (to learn) also follow this pattern.

Finding verbs in a dictionary can sometimes be a challenge, because the word listed can look quite different from the one you were looking for. This section will show you how to look up verbs in your French–English dictionary and how to handle some common difficulties. If you don't have a dictionary, you can use the **Points de référence** at the back of this *Coursebook*.

## [1] LOOKING UP VERBS

Imagine you want to say:

'I'm watching the football. My team is winning!'

You will not find 'watching' and 'winning' in the dictionary, because in dictionaries, verbs are listed only in their *infinitive* form. So 'watching' and 'winning' would appear as '(to) watch' and '(to) win'. The dictionary entries would look something like this:

> **watch** *n* montre *f* ♦ *v* regarder

> **win** *n* (*in sports etc*) victoire *f* ♦ *v* gagner

If more than one French meaning is given, ensure that you've chosen the verb by checking that it has the 'verb' label. Depending on the dictionary, this could appear as *verb, vb, v, vi* or *vt*.

> Which words would you look up to find the verbs in these sentences?
> 'He often goes to Montreal.'
> 'She sang beautifully.'

### Verbs in the French–English section

Imagine you were looking for the meaning of the verb **porte** in this sentence:

**La femme porte un sac.**

Again, you would have to look for it in its *infinitive* form: **porter**. Make sure you're found the infinitive by checking:

- that it ends in **–er, –ir** or **–re**
- that it is labelled *verb, vb, v, vi* or *vt*
- that its meaning makes sense in the context

Which of these entries relates to the verb in the sentence above?

> **porte** *nf* door
> **porter** *v* to carry; to wear
> **porteur** *nm* porter

> Now test your dictionary skills by doing the related activity on page 3 of your *Workbook*.

## [2] REGULAR OR IRREGULAR?

Suppose you want to say:

'We always take the train. Mum usually loses her ticket.'

You know how to find the verbs in their infinitive form '(to) take' and '(to) lose', but how can you tell if they are regular or irregular?

Dictionaries vary in the way they show irregular verbs.

- The **Points de référence** section in this *Coursebook* uses different symbols to indicate whether a verb is regular *, semi-regular ** or irregular ✢, but not all dictionaries do this.

- Some dictionaries list the conjugations of common irregular verbs in a separate section at the front or back of the dictionary, something like the one on page 51 of this *Coursebook*.

- Other dictionaries show that a verb is irregular by including the conjugations after the infinitive, like this:

> **être** *v* (*pr. ind.* **je suis, tu es, il est, n. sommes, v. êtes, ils sont**) to be

If a dictionary doesn't indicate that a verb is irregular, you can usually assume it is regular.

> Look up the irregular verb **être** to see how it is listed in your dictionary. Does your dictionary have a separate section for irregular verbs?

> Find out whether the verbs **mettre** and **entendre** are regular or irregular.

> Now test your dictionary skills by doing the related activity on page 13 of your *Workbook*.

# [3] ADAPTING DICTIONARY INFORMATION

Imagine you want to say:

'She is waiting in the café. They look at the menu. He chooses a sandwich. She wants an icecream.'

For each sentence, you need to:

1. identify the verb and convert it to infinitive form
2. look up the infinitive in the dictionary to find its French equivalent
3. check if the verb is regular or irregular
4. conjugate the verb correctly

   For regular verbs, this means dropping the **–er**, **–re** or **–ir** from the infinitive and adding the appropriate ending. Irregular verbs need to be checked individually.

For example:

|  | 1 Identify the verb and convert it to infinitive form | 2 Look up the infinitive in the dictionary to find its French equivalent | 3 Check if the verb is regular or irregular | 4 Conjugate the verb correctly |
|---|---|---|---|---|
| She is waiting in the café. | (to) wait | **attendre** | regular **–re** | **elle attend** |
| They look at the menu. | (to) look at | **regarder** | regular **–er** | **ils regardent** |
| He chooses a sandwich. | (to) choose | **choisir** | regular **–ir** | **il choisit** |
| She wants an icecream. | (to) want | **vouloir** | irregular | **elle veut** |

▶ Work through the same process with these sentences: 'I always confuse the twins. They're growing up. They work at the supermarket now.'

▶ Now test your dictionary skills by doing the related activity on page 23 of your *Workbook*.

# [4] ADAPTING REFLEXIVE VERBS

Sometimes when you use a dictionary to look up a verb, you find the French infinitive is preceded by **se** or **s'**. This indicates that the verb is *reflexive* and that there are *two* things to consider when conjugating:

• the appropriate *verb ending*
• the appropriate *reflexive pronoun*

Suppose you want to say:

We are settling into the new house.

I am settling into the new house.

Having found the infinitive **s'installer**, you would need to adapt it as follows:

**Nous nous installons dans la nouvelle maison.**
**Je m'installe dans la nouvelle maison.**

▶ Find the French for 'to wonder'. How would you change the infinitive for these sentences?
'You're wondering whether it's dad?'
'She's wondering whether it's dad, too.'

▶ Now test your dictionary skills by doing the related activity on page 35 of your *Workbook*.

n = noun  m = masculine  f = feminine  pl = plural  v = verb  prep = preposition  adj = adjective  inv = invariable  fam = familiar

\* = regular verb (see page 50)    \*\* = semi-regular –er verb (see page 51)    ✤ = irregular verb (see page 51)

## A

**à**  at; in; to
**à bientôt !**  see you soon!
**à côté (de)**  prep next to, beside
**à demain !**  see you tomorrow!
**à droite (de)**  prep to the right (of)
**à faire**  to do
**à gauche (de)**  prep to the left (of)
**à ... heures**  at ... o'clock
**à la page**  on page ...
**à qui**  to whom, whose
**l'homme à la barbe blanche**  the man with the white beard
**abricot**  nm apricot
**accent**  nm accent
**accompagner\***  v to accompany
**d'accord**  OK, I agree
**être d'accord**  to agree
**acheter\*\***  v to buy
**acteur**  nm, **actrice**  nf actor
**actif, active**  adj active
**addition**  nf bill
**adjectif**  nm adjective
**adorable**  adj gorgeous, adorable
**adorer\***  v to love, to adore
**adulte**  adj adult
**aérobique**  nf aerobics
**aéroport**  nm airport
**affectueux, affectueuse**  adj affectionate
**âge**  nm age
**elle a quel âge ?**  how old is she?
**tu as quel âge ?**  how old are you?
**ah**  ah
**ah bon ?**  oh really?
**aïe !**  ouch!
**aimer\***  v to like; to love
**air**  nm air

**aller✤**  v to go
**aller-retour**  nm return ticket
**aller simple**  nm one-way ticket
**allez (les) ... !**  come on (the) ... !
**allons-y !**  let's go!
**ça te va bien !**  it suits you!
**j'y vais**  I'm going, I'm off
**on y va**  let's go
**pour aller à ... ?**  how do I get to ... ?
**va-t-en !**  go away!
**allô**  hello (on the telephone)
**alors**  then, well then
**et alors ?**  so?, so what?
**Amérindiens**  nmpl native Canadians
**ami**  nm, **amie**  nf friend
**amusant(e)**  adj amusing, funny
**s'amuser\***  v to enjoy oneself, to have fun
**an**  nm year
**j'ai treize ans**  I am thirteen (years old)
**ananas**  nm pineapple
**anglais**  nm English (language)
**animal**  nm, **animaux**  npl animal
**anniversaire**  nm birthday
**annoncer\***  v to announce
**août**  nm August
**appartement**  nm apartment
**s'appeler\*\***  v to be called
**je m'appelle**  my name is
**tu t'appelles comment ?**  what's your name?
**apprendre✤**  v to learn
**aprèm**  nm fam arvo
**après**  prep after
**après-midi**  nm afternoon
**cet après-midi**  this afternoon

**arrêter\***  v to stop
**arrivée**  nf arrival
**arriver\***  v to arrive, to come
**asperges**  nfpl asparagus
**aspirateur**  nm vacuum
**assez**  rather, fairly, enough
**je suis assez grand**  I am fairly tall
**assiette**  nf plate
**athlétisme**  nm athletics
**attaque**  nf attack
**attendre\***  v to wait (for)
**attente**  nf wait
**attention**  nf attention, care
**attention !**  watch out!
**attention à ...**  watch out for ...
**faites attention !**  be careful!
**attentivement**  carefully
**au revoir**  goodbye
**aujourd'hui**  today
**aussi**  also, too
**aussi ... que**  as ... as
**moi aussi**  me too
**Australie**  nf Australia
**Australien**  nm, **Australienne**  nf Australian (person)
**australien(ne)**  adj Australian
**automne**  nm autumn
**autre**  adj other
**avant**  prep before
**avec**  prep with
**et avec ça ?**  and with that?, anything else?
**avion**  nm aeroplane
**avocat**  nm avocado; lawyer
**avoir✤**  v to have
**avoir faim**  to be hungry
**avoir soif**  to be thirsty
**j'ai douze ans**  I am twelve (years old)

## B

**babyfoot**  nm table football
**badminton**  nm badminton

**bagage**  nm luggage, baggage
**baguette**  nf bread stick
**bain**  nm bath
**balcon**  nm balcony
**ballon**  nm ball
**banane**  nf banana
**bande**  nf **dessinée** comic strip
**banque**  nf bank
**barbe**  nf beard
**base-ball**  nm baseball
**basket-ball**  nm basketball
**baskets**  nmpl sneakers
**bâton**  nm **de colle**  gluestick
**beau (bel), belle, beaux**  adj lovely; beautiful
**beaucoup**  lots, a lot, much, many
**ben ...**  well ...
**berk !**  yuk!
**beurre**  nm butter
**bibliothèque**  nf library
**bien**  well
**bien sûr**  of course
**bientôt**  soon
**à bientôt**  see you soon
**billard**  nm billiards
**billet**  nm ticket
**billeterie**  nf **automatique** ticket machine
**biscuit**  nm biscuit
**bise**  nf kiss on cheeks (French greeting)
**bizarre**  adj weird, bizarre
**blanc(he)**  adj white
**bleu(e)**  adj blue
**bleu marine**  adj inv navy blue
**blond(e)**  adj blond
**blouson**  nm jacket
**boire**  v to drink
**boisson**  nf drink
**bon, bonne**  adj good
**ah bon ?**  oh, really?
**bonne idée !**  good idea!
**bonne nuit**  good night
**en bonne forme**  fit
**bonbon**  nm lolly, sweet

**bonjour** hello, good morning, good afternoon

**bonsoir** good evening

**botte** *nf* boot

**bouc** *nm* goatee; billy goat

**boucherie** *nf* butcher's shop

**bouger**\*\* *v* to move

**boulangerie** *nf* bakery

**boule** *nf* ball

**boutique** *nf* **d'animaux** pet shop

**braderie** *nf* discount centre

**bravo !** well done!

il y a du **brouillard** it is foggy

**brousse** *nf* bush

**brun(e)** *adj* brown

**buanderie** *nf* laundry (room)

**bureau** *nm* office

**bureau de tabac** *nm* shop selling tobacco, stamps and tickets

**bus** *nm* bus

**but** *nm* goal

# C

**ça** this, that

**ça alors !** really! you don't say!

**ça fait ...** that makes ...

**ça m'est égal** I don't mind, its all the same to me

**ça te va bien !** it suits you!

**ça va** things are OK, I'm well

**c'est ça** that's right

**cacatoès** *nm* cockatoo

**café** *nm* café; coffee

**café au lait** coffee with milk

**cahier** *nm* exercise book

**caleçon** *nm* boxer shorts

**(néo-)calédonien(ne)** *adj* New Caledonian

**calme** *adj* calm

**du calme !** calm down!

**Canada** *nm* Canada

**Canadien** *nm*, **Canadienne** *nf* Canadian (person)

**canapé** *nm* couch, sofa

**cantine** *nf* canteen, tuckshop

**capable** *adj* able, capable

**carotte** *nf* carrot

**carte** *nf* card; map; menu

**carte de crédit** credit card

**carte postale** postcard

**casquette** *nf* cap

**cathédrale** *nf* cathedral

**ce (cet), cette, ces** this/that, these/those

**célèbre** *adj* famous

**cellier** *nm* storeroom

**centre** *nm* **communautaire** community centre

**centre ville** *nm* city centre, town centre

**certain(e)** *adj* certain

**c'est** it's, that's

**c'est ça** that's right

**c'est nul !** *fam* that's pathetic!, that's so dumb!

**c'est tout** that's all

**c'est trop fort, ça !** *fam* that's pushing it!

**chaleur** *nf* heat

**chambre** *nf* bedroom

**champignon** *nm* mushroom

**chance** *nf* luck

**bonne chance !** good luck!

**changer**\*\* *v* to change

**chant** *nm* chant, song

**chapeau** *nm* hat

**chaque** *adj* each

**charcuterie** *nf* pork butcher's shop and delicatessen

**chat** *nm* cat

**châtain(e)** *adj* chestnut brown

**château** *nm* castle

**chaud(e)** *adj* hot

**chaussette** *nf* sock

**chaussure** *nf* shoe

**chauve** *adj* bald

**chef** *nm* leader; chef

**chemise** *nf* shirt

**cher, chère** *adj* expensive; dear

**chercher**\* *v* to look for

**va chercher !** go fetch!

**cheval** *nm*, **chevaux** *nmpl* horse

**cheveux** *nmpl* hair

**cheveux en brosse** crew cut, spiky hair

**chez (moi)** at (my) place

**chic** *adj inv* stylish, smart

**chien** *nm*, **chienne** *nf* dog

**chiot** *nm* puppy

**chocolat** *nm* chocolate

**chocolat chaud** hot chocolate

**choisir**\* *v* to choose

**choix** *nm* choice

**chose** *nf* thing

**chouette !** *fam* great!

**chut !** sshh!

**ciao** *fam* bye

**ci-joint(e)** *adj* attached, enclosed

**ciné(ma)** *nm* cinema

**cinq** five

**cinquante** fifty

**cinquième** *adj* fifth

**citadelle** *nf* citadel

**citron** *nm* lemon

**citrouille** *nf* pumpkin

**classe** *nf* class

**classeur** *nm* ring binder

**classique** *adj* classic(al)

**client** *nm*, **cliente** *nf* client

**coca(-cola)** *nm* Coca-Cola

**cochon** *nm* pig

**cocotier** *nm* coconut palm

**collant** *nm* stockings, tights, pantyhose

**collier** *nm* necklace

**combien ?** how much?; how many?

**c'est combien?** how much is it?

**comme** as; like

**comme ci comme ça** so-so; it's OK

**comme d'habitude** as usual

**commencer**\*\* *v* to begin, to start

**comment** how, what

**il est comment ?** what is he/it like?

**tu es comment ?** what do you look like?

**tu t'appelles comment ?** what's your name?

**commerçant** *nm*, **commerçante** *nf* shopkeeper

**commerce** *nm* business

**petit commerce** small business

**commissariat** *nm* police station

**compagnon** *nm* companion

**compétition** *nf* competition

**complet, complète** *adj* whole

**composter**\* *v* to validate (a ticket)

**comprendre**\* *v* to understand

**concert** *nm* concert

**concombre** *nm* cucumber

**conducteur** *nm*, **conductrice** *nf* driver

**confiture** *nf* jam

**confortable** *adj* comfortable

**connexion** *nf* **culturelle** cultural connection

**content(e)** *adj* happy

**continuer**\* *nm* to continue

**contrôleur**\* *v* conductor

**copain** *nm*, **copine** *nf* friend

**correspondant** *m*, **correspondante** *nf* penfriend, penpal

**correspondre**\* **(avec)** *v* to correspond (with); to write to

**costume** *nm* costume; suit

**côté** *nm* side

**à côté (de)** *prep* next to, beside

**couleur** *nf* colour

**couloir** *nm* aisle

**courage !** cheer up!; be brave!

**courgette** *nf* zucchini

**courses** *nfpl* shopping

**court(e)** *adj* short

**cousin** *nm*, **cousine** *nf* cousin

**couteau** *nm* knife

**couvert(e)** *adj* covered

**crayon** *nm* pencil

**crémerie** *nf* dairy

**croissant** *nm* croissant

**cuillère** *nf* spoon

**cuisine** *nf* kitchen; cooking

**faire la cuisine** *v* to do the cooking

**culture** *nf* culture

**cybercafé** *nm* Internet café

**cyclone** *nm* cyclone

# D

**dame** *nf* lady

**dangereux, dangereuse** *adj* dangerous

**dans** in

**danseur** *nm*, **danseuse** *nf* dancer

**de, d'** of, from

**de ... à ...** from ... to ...

**débardeur** *nm* tank top, singlet

**décembre** *nm* December

**décider**\* *v* to decide

**décorer**\* *v* to decorate

**dégoûtant(e)** *adj* disgusting

**degré** *nm* degree
  **il fait … degré(s)**
  it is … degree(s)
**déjà** already
**déjeuner** *nm* lunch
**déjeuner** *v* to have lunch
**délicieux, délicieuse** *adj*
  delicious
**demain** tomorrow
  **à demain !** see you
  tomorrow!
**demander\*** *v* to ask
**demi-tour** *nm* U-turn
**départ** *nm* departure
se **dépêcher\*** *v* to hurry
**depuis** since
**derrière** *prep* behind
**des** some; any
**descendre\*** *v* to go down
  **descendre de** to get out
  of (a vehicle)
**descente** *nf* downward
  slope
**description** *nf* description
**désirer\*** *v* to want, to wish
  **qu'est-ce que vous
  désirez ?** what would
  you like?
**désolé(e)** *adj* sorry
  **je suis désolé(e)**
  I'm sorry
**dessert** *nm* dessert
**dessin** *nm* drawing
**détester\*** *v* to hate
**deux** two
**deuxième** *adj* second
**devant** *prep* in front (of)
**deviner\*** *v* to guess
  **devinez !** guess what!
**devoirs** *nmpl* homework
**dialogue** *nm* dialogue
**dictionnaire** *nm* dictionary
**différent(e)** *adj* different
**difficile** *adj* difficult
**dimanche** *nm* Sunday
**dîner** *nm* dinner
**dîner\*** *v* to dine (evening
  meal)
**dingue** *adj* crazy
**directeur** *nm*, **directrice** *nf*
  director
se **disputer\*** *v* to argue
**dix** ten
**dix-huit** eighteen
**docteur** *nm* doctor
**donner\*** *v* to give
**drap** *nm* sheet
**droit** straight
  **tout droit** straight
  ahead

**droite** *nf* right
  **à droite (de)** to the
  right (of)

# E

**eau** *nf* **minérale** mineral
  water
**échange** *nm* exchange
  **échange scolaire**
  student exchange
**écouter\*** *v* to listen (to)
**écrivez … !** write … !
**égal(e)** *adj* equal
  **ça m'est égal** I don't
  mind, it's all the same
  to me
**église** *nf* church
**élégance** *nf* elegance
**élégant(e)** *adj* elegant
**elle** she; it
**e-mail** *nm* email
**en** in, by
  **en avion/bus/train**
  by aeroplane/bus/train
  **en cours de …** in the
  process of …
  **en face (de)** *prep*
  opposite, facing
  **en plein air** outdoors
**encore** still; again; yet
**enfant** *nmf* child
**enfin** at last
**ennuyeux, ennuyeuse** *adj*
  boring
**énorme** *adj* huge
**ensemble** together
**entendre\*** *v* to hear
**entouré(e) de** surrounded by
**entraînement** *nm* training
**entrée** *nf* entrance
**enveloppé(e)** *adj* wrapped
**envoyer\*\*** *v* to send
**épicerie** *nf* general store,
  milk bar (Aus), dairy (NZ)
**EPS (l'éducation** *f* **physique
  et sportive)** PE (physical
  education)
**équipe** *nf* team
**équitation** *nf* horse-riding
**erreur** *nf* mistake
**escalier** *nm* staircase, stairs
**escrime** *nf* fencing
**espérer\*\*** *v* to hope
  **j'espère que oui !**
  I hope so!
**essence** *nf* petrol
**est-ce que … ?** is it that … ?
  **est-ce que tu
  t'appelles Chloé ?**
  is your name Chloe?

**et** and
**étage** *nm* floor, storey
**été** *nm* summer
**éternité** *nf* eternity
  **ça fait une éternité
  qu'on attend !**
  we've been waiting
  for ages!
**être** *v* to be
**euh …** um …
**euro** *nm* euro (European
  Union currency)
s'**exclamer\*** *v* to exclaim
s'**excuser\*** *v* to apologise
  **excusez-moi** excuse me
**exemple** *nm* example
  **par exemple** for
  example
**expérience** *nf* experience
**expliquer\*** *v* to explain
**expression** *nf* expression
à l'**extérieur** *nm* outside

# F

**facile** *adj* easy
**faim** *nf* hunger
**fainéant(e)** *adj fam* slack, lazy
**faire** *v* to do; to make
  **faire la tournée** to do
  the rounds (of)
  **faire les courses**
  to do the shopping
  **fais comme chez toi !**
  make yourself at home!
  **il fait beau** it is nice
  weather
  **il fait … degré(s)** it is
  degree(s)
  **il fait mauvais** it is bad
  weather
**famille** *nf* family
  **famille d'accueil**
  host family
**fantôme** *nm* ghost
**fascinant(e)** *adj* fascinating
**fatigant(e)** *adj* tiring
**fatigué(e)** *adj* tired
il **faut** it is necessary;
  we/you must/need to/
  have to
**félicitations** *nfpl*
  congratulations
**féliciter\*** *v* to
  congratulate
**femelle** *nf* female
**femme** *nf* woman; wife
**fenêtre** *nf* window
**fermer\*** *v* to close
**féroce** *adj* ferocious

**fêter\*** *v* to celebrate
**feu** *nm* traffic light; fire
**fille** *nf* girl; daughter
**fils** *nm* son
**finalement** finally
**finir\*** *v* to finish
**fleur** *nf* flower
**fleuriste** *nmf* florist
**fois** *nf* time
  **une fois** once
**fonction** *nf* function
**forme** *nf* shape
  **en bonne forme** fit
**formidable** *adj* great
**fort(e)** *adj* strong
**fortifié(e)** *adj* fortified
**fourchette** *nf* fork
**foyer** *nm* home
**frais, fraîche** *adj* cool;
  fresh
**fraise** *nf* strawberry
**franc** *nm* franc (currency
  of New Caledonia)
**français** *nm* French
  (language)
**Français** *nm*, **Française** *nf*
  French (person)
**France** *f* France
**frère** *nm* brother
**frisé(e)** *adj* curly
**froid(e)** *adj* cold
**fromage** *nm* cheese
**fromagerie** *nf* cheese shop
**fruit** *nm* fruit
**fumé(e)** *adj* smoked
**fumeur** smoking

# G

**gagner\*** *v* to win
**garage** *nm* garage
**garçon** *nm* boy
**gare** *nf* train station
  **gare des autobus**
  bus station,
  central bus stop (NZ)
**gauche** *nf* left
  **à gauche (de)** *prep* to the
  left (of)
**gaufre** *nf* waffle
**gendarmerie** *nf* police
  station
en **général** usually,
  generally
**génial !** great!
**gentil(le)** *adj* kind; nice
**glace** *nf* ice-cream
**goinfre** *nm fam* greedy
  guts, pig
**gomme** *nf* eraser

**grand(e)** *adj* big, tall
  **pas grand-chose** not much
**grande surface** *nf* hypermarket
**grand-mère** *nf* grandmother
**grands-parents** *nmpl* grandparents
**grand-père** *nm* grandfather
**grillé(e)** *adj* grilled
**gris(e)** *adj* grey
**gros(se)** *adj* big, fat
  **gros malin !** *fam* you're a bright one!
**groupe** *nm* group
**guichet** *nm* ticket office
**guider\*** *v* to guide
**guillemet** *mn* quotation mark
**gymnase** *nm* gymnasium

# H

**s'habiller\*** *v* to dress (oneself)
**d'habitude** usually
**harnais** *nm* harness
**haut-parleur** *nm* loud speaker
**hein ?** huh?
**heure** *nf* time, o'clock, hour
  **à deux heures** at two o'clock
  **à quelle heure ?** at what time ?
  **il est deux heures** it is two o'clock
  **il est quelle heure ?** what time is it?
**hip hip hip hourra !** *fam* hip hip hurrah!
**histoire** *nf* history
**histoire-géo(graphie)** *nf* social studies, society and environment, SOSE, HSIE, history-geography
**hiver** *nm* winter
**hockey** *nm* **sur glace** ice-hockey
**homme** *nm* man
**hôpital** *nm* hospital
**horrible** *adj* horrible
**hostile** *adj* hostile
**hôtel** *nm* hotel
  **hôtel de ville** town hall
**husky** *nm*, **huskies** *nmpl* husky (dog)
**hypermarché** *nm* hypermarket

# I

**ici** here
**idée** *nf* idea
**il** he; it
**il y a** there is, there are
  **il y a du soleil** it is sunny
**impatience** *nf* impatience
**impatient(e)** *adj* impatient
**imper(méable)** *nm* raincoat
**important(e)** *adj* important
**impossible** *adj* impossible
**inflammable** *adj* flammable
**information** *nf* information
**inspecter\*** *v* to inspect
**inspecteur** *nm*, **inspectrice** *nf* inspector
**s'installer\*** *v* to settle in(to)
**intelligent(e)** *adj* intelligent
**intéressant(e)** *adj* interesting
**internet** *nm* Internet
**intersection** *nf* intersection
**inviter\*** *v* to invite
  **être invité à se présenter à …** to be asked to come to …

# J

**ne … jamais** never
**jambon** *nm* ham
**jardin** *nm* garden
**jaune** *adj* yellow
**je** I
  **j'en ai marre** *fam* I am fed up, I am sick of it
  **je ne sais pas** I don't know
**j'y vais** I'm going, I'm off
**jean** *nm* jeans
**jeu** *nm*, **jeux** *nmpl* game
  **jeu de rôle** role-play
  **jeux video** video games
  **salle** *nf* **de jeux** arcade (video games)
**jeudi** *nm* Thursday
**jeune** *adj* young
  **les jeunes** *nmfpl* young people
**jour** *nm* day
  **tous les jours** every day
**jouer\*** *v* to play
  **jouer à la pétanque** to play pétanque
  **jouer au hockey** to play hockey
  **jouer aux boules** to play boules

**journée** *nf* day
**jumeau** *nm*, **jumelle** *nf*, **jumeaux** *nmpl* twin(s)
**jupe** *nf* skirt
**jus** *nm* juice
**juste** *adj* fair
  **ce n'est pas juste !** it's not fair!

# K L

**karaté** *nm* karate
**kayak** *nm* kayak
**kilo** *nm* kilogram
**kiwi** *nm* kiwi fruit
**l', la, le, les** the
**là** there
**là-bas** over there
**laisser\*** *v* to let, to allow
**lait** *nm* milk
**langue** *nf* language; tongue
**latin** *nm* Latin
**laver\*** *v* to wash
  **se laver\*** *v* to wash oneself, to have a wash
**leader** *nm* leader
**légume** *nm* vegetable
**librairie** *nf* bookshop
**libre-service** *nm* self-service
**limonade** *nf* lemonade
**livre** *nm* book
**loin (de)** *prep* far (from)
**long, longue** *adj* long
**lundi** *nm* Monday
**lunettes** *nfpl* **de soleil** sunglasses
**lycée** *nm* senior secondary school (15–18 years old)

# M

**ma** *see* **mon**
**machine** *nf* machine
**madame** *nf* (**Mme**) madam (Mrs, Ms)
**mademoiselle** *nf* (**Mlle**) miss (Miss, Ms)
**magasin** *nm* shop
**magnifique** *adj* magnificent
**maillot** *nm* **de bain** bathers, swimsuit, togs
**maintenant** now
**mairie** *nf* town hall
**mais** but
**maison** *nf* house
**maître** *nm* master
**majorité** *nf* majority

**mal** badly, not well
  **pas mal** not bad
**malamute** *nm* malamute (dog)
**manger\*\*** *v* to eat
**mangue** *nf* mango
**marche** *nf* walking
**marché** *nm* market
**marcher\*** *v* to walk
**mardi** *nm* Tuesday
**mari** *nm* husband
**marrant(e)** *adj* funny
**j'en ai marre !** *fam* I am fed up!
**marron** *adj inv* brown
**masque** *nm* mask
**masseur** *nm*, **masseuse** *nf* masseur
**match** *nm* match
**mathémathiques** *nfpl* mathematics
**maths** *nfpl fam* maths
**matière** *nf* subject
**matin** *nm* morning
  **du matin** in the morning
**mauvais(e)** *adj* bad
**méchant(e)** *adj* nasty, naughty
**melon** *nm* melon
**même** even; same
**ménage** *nm* housework
**merci** thank you
**mercredi** *nm* Wednesday
**mère** *nf* mother
**mes** *see* **mon**
**météo** *nf* weather forecast
**méthode** *nf* method
**mettre** *v* to put
**mi** *adj* half, mid
  **mi-long, mi-longue** *adj* mid-length
**miam !** yum!
**midi** *nm* midday
**mignon(ne)** *adj* cute
**mince** ♦ *fam* damn ♦ *adj* slim, thin
  **je suis mince** I am slim
**minuit** *nm* midnight
**minute** *nf* minute
**misérable** *adj* miserable
**mission** *nf* mission
**moche** *adj fam* ugly
**moderne** *adj* modern
**moi** me
  **moi aussi** me too
  **moi non plus** me neither
**moins** minus; less
  **moins … que** less … than

**mois** *nm* month

**mon, ma, mes** my

**monde** *nm* world

   **tout le monde** everyone

**monsieur** *nm* (**M.**) sir, gentleman, (Mr)

**monstre** *nm* monster

**monter*** *v* to go up; to get on (bus, etc.)

**Montréal** *n* Montreal

**mot** *nm* word

**moustache** *nf* moustache

**moyen(ne)** *adj* average, medium

**mur** *nm* wall

**musée** *nm* museum

**musical(e)** *adj* musical

**musique** *nf* music

# N

**natation** *nf* swimming

**ne ... pas** not, do not

   **je ne sais pas** I don't know

**n'est-ce pas ?** isn't it?

   **ils sont chers, n'est-ce pas ?** they are expensive, aren't they?

   **il aime la télé, n'est-ce pas ?** he likes TV, doesn't he?

**neige** *nf* snow

   **il neige** it is snowing

**nerveusement** nervously

**Noël** *nm* Christmas

**noir(e)** *adj* black

**noix** *nf* **de coco** coconut

**nom** *nm* name

   **nom de famille** family name, surname

**nombre** *nm* number

**non** no

   **non-fumeur** non-smoking

**normalement** usually

**notre, nos** our

**Nouméa** *n* Noumea

**nous** we

**nouveau (nouvel), nouvelle, nouveaux** *adj* new

**Nouvelle-Calédonie** *nf* New Caledonia

**nouvelles** *nfpl* news

**novembre** *nm* November

**nul(le)** *adj* worthless, pathetic

   **c'est nul !** *fam* it's pathetic!

**numéro** *nm* number

# O

**occupé(e)** *adj* taken; busy

**octobre** *nm* October

**œil** *nm* eye

   **mon œil !** *fam* you're pulling my leg!, I don't believe you!

**œuf** *nm* egg

**office** *nm* **du tourisme** tourist office

**offrir** *v* to offer

**oie** *nf* goose

**oignon** *nm* onion

**oiseau** *nm*, **oiseaux** *nmpl* bird

**on** we, one, people

   **on y va** let's go

**ondulé(e)** *adj* wavy

**onze** eleven

**orange** ♦ *adj inv* orange ♦ *nf* orange

**ordre** *nm* order

**originaire (de)** *adj* native (to)

**ou** or

**où** where

**oublier*** *v* to forget

**oui** yes

**oups !** oops!

**ouvert(e)** *adj* open

**ouvrir** *v* to open

# P

**page** *nf* page

**pain** *nm* bread

   **pain complet** wholemeal bread

**pantalon** *nm* trousers, pants

**papa** *nm* Dad

**papeterie** *nf* stationery shop

**parc** *nm* park

**parce que** because

**pardon** I'm sorry, I beg your pardon, excuse me

**parent** *nm* parent

**paresseux, paresseuse** *adj* lazy

**parfait(e)** *adj* perfect

**parler*** *v* to speak

**participer*** **à** *v* to take part (in), to participate (in)

**partir** *v* to leave

**pas** not

   **pas du tout** not at all

   **pas encore** not yet

   **pas grand-chose** not much

   **pas question !** no way!

**passager** *nm* **passagère** *nf* passenger

**passer*** *v* to pass (by); to spend (time)

   **passer l'aspirateur** to do the vacuuming

   **passer le week-end** to spend the weekend

**pâtes** *nfpl* pasta

**patience** *nf* patience

**patient(e)** *adj* patient

**patinoire** *nf* ice-skating rink

**pâtisserie** *nf* cake, pastry; cake shop

**pauvre** *adj* poor

**pêche** *nf* fishing

**pendant** during

**penser*** *v* to think

**perdre*** *v* to lose

**perdu(e)** *adj* lost

**père** *nm* father

**permanent(e)** *adj* permanent

**personne** *nf* person

**personnalisé(e)** *adj* personalised

**pétanque** *nf* petanque

**petit(e)** *adj* small, little

   **petit commerce** *nm* small business

   **petit-déjeuner** *nm* breakfast

un **peu** a little

**peut-être** perhaps, maybe

**pharmacie** *nf* chemist, pharmacy

**photo** *nf* photo

**pièce** *nf* room

   **la pièce** each

**piéton** *nm* pedestrian

**pique-nique** *nm* picnic

**piscine** *nf* swimming pool

**place** *nf* town square; seat

   **place côté couloir** aisle seat

   **place côté fenêtre** window seat

**plage** *nf* beach

**plaisir** *nm* pleasure

   **avec plaisir** with pleasure

s'il te **plaît**, **s'il vous plaît** please

**plan** *nm* map

**planer*** *v fam* to dream

   **tu planes !** you're dreaming!

**plein tarif** *nm* full fare

il **pleut** it is raining

**plus** more

   **de plus en plus** more and more

   **moi non plus** me neither

   **plus ... que** more ... than

   **plus tard** later

**point** *nm* point

   **points de langue** language points

   **points de prononciation** pronunciation points

   **points de référence** reference points

**poire** *nf* pear

**poisson** *nm* fish

**poissonnerie** *nf* fish shop

**pomme** *nf* apple

**pomme de terre** *nf* potato

**populaire** *adj* popular

**port** *nm* port, harbour

**porte** *nf* door, gate

**porter*** *v* to wear, to carry

**possible** *adj* possible

**poste** ♦ *nf* post office ♦ *nm* job; position

**poste** *nm* **de police** police station

**pouah !** yuk!

**poulet** *nm* chicken

**pour** for; in order to

**pourquoi** why

**pratique** *adj* practical

**préféré(e)** *adj* favourite, preferred

**préférer*** *v* to prefer

**premier, première** *adj* first

**prendre** *v* to take

**préparer*** *v* to prepare

**près (de)** *prep* near

   **tout près (de)** very near

**présenter*** *v* to introduce

   **je te présente ...** I'd like to introduce you to ...

   **se présenter*** *v* to introduce oneself

**pressé(e)** *adj* in a hurry

je vous en **prie** you're welcome; please do

**produit** *nm* product

**prof(esseur)** *nmf* teacher

**promenade** *nf* walk

**prononcer*** *v* to pronounce

**prononciation** *nf* pronunciation

**propriétaire** *nmf* owner

**provisions** *nfpl* provisions, food

**puis** then

**pull(-over)** *nm* jumper, jersey
**pyjama** *nm* pyjamas

# Q

**qu'est-ce que ... ?** what ...?
  **qu'est-ce que c'est ?** what's that? what is it?
  **qu'est-ce que vous prenez ?** what are you having?
**quand** when
**quarante** forty
**quatorze** fourteen
**quatre** four
**quatre-vingts** eighty
**que** than
  **moins cher que ...** cheaper than ...
**Québec** *nm* Quebec
**Québécois** *nm*, **Québécoise** *nf* person from Quebec
**québécois(e)** *adj* from Quebec
**quel(le)** what, which
  **il est quelle heure ?** what time is it?
  **quel temps fait-il ?** what is the weather like?
  **quelle surprise !** what a surprise!
**quelquefois** sometimes
**quelqu'un** someone, somebody
**question** *nf* question
**queue** *nf* tail; queue
**qui** who
  **c'est à qui ?** whose is it?
  **qui est-ce ?** who is (it)?, who's that?
**quincaillerie** *nf* hardware store
**quinze** fifteen
**quitter*** *v* to leave
**quoi** what

# R

**raide** *adj* straight
**randonnée** *nf* bushwalking
**ranger**** *v* to tidy
**rap** *m* rap (music)
**rapide** *adj* fast
**rare** *adj* rare
**rarement** rarely
**rasant(e)** *adj fam* boring
en **réalité** in fact

**recherche** *nf* search, research
**reconnaître** *v* to recognise
**récré(ation)** *nf* recess
**regarder*** *v* to look at
**règle** *nf* ruler
**remonter*** *v* to go back up
**remparts** *nmpl* fortified walls
**remplir*** *v* to fill
**rencontrer*** *v* to meet
  **se rencontrer*** *v* to meet each other
**rentrée** *nf* start of the new school year
**répéter**** *v* to repeat
**répondre*** *v* to answer
**réponse** *nf* answer
**réseau** *nm* network
**ressembler* à** *v* to resemble, to look like
**restaurant** *nm* restaurant
**rester*** *v* to stay
en **retard** late
**retourner*** *v* to return
se **réveiller*** *v* to wake up
au **revoir** goodbye
**rez-de-chaussée** *nm* ground floor
**riz** *nm* rice
**robe** *nf* dress
**roller** *nm* in-line skating
**romantique** *adj* romantic
**rose** *adj* pink
**rouge** *adj* red
**rougir*** *v* to blush
en **route** on the way, on the road
**roux, rousse** *adj* red-haired
**royal(e)** *adj* royal
**rue** *nf* street
**rugby** *nm* rugby
**rumsteak** *nm* rump steak

# S

**sa** *see* **son**
**sac** *nm* bag
je ne **sais** pas I don't know
**saison** *nf* season
**salade** *nf* salad; lettuce
**salle** *nf* room
  **salle à manger** dining room
  **salle d'attente** waiting room
  **salle de bain** bathroom
  **salle de jeux** arcade (video games)
  **salle de séjour** family room, living room

**samedi** *nm* Saturday
**salon** *nm* lounge room
**salut** hi
**sandale** *nf* sandal
**sandwich** *nm* sandwich
**saumon** *nm* salmon
**science** *nf* science
  **sciences naturelles** natural sciences (biology)
  **sciences physiques** physical sciences (chemistry, physics)
**scolaire** *adj* school
  **échange scolaire** student exchange
**sculpter*** *v* to sculpt, to carve
**semaine** *nf* week
**sembler*** *v* to seem
**sept** seven
**serpent** *nm* snake
**serviette** *nf* **(de bain)** (bath) towel
**serviette** *nf* **(de table)** napkin, serviette
**ses** *see* **son**
**seul(e)** *adj* alone
**seulement** only
**shopping** *nm* shopping
**short** *nm* shorts
**si** yes; if
**signal** *nm* signal
**silence** *nm* silence
**simple** *adj* simple
**sirop** *nm* **d'érable** maple syrup
**six** six
**skate** *nm* skate-boarding
**ski** *nm* skiing
  **faire du ski** *v* to go skiing
  **ski de randonnée** cross-country skiing
  **ski nautique** waterskiing
**slip** *nm* underpants
**sœur** *nf* sister
**soif** *nf* thirst
**soir** *nm* evening
  **du soir** in the evening
**soixante** sixty
**soleil** *nm* sun
**solution** *nf* solution
**son, sa, ses** his, her, its, one's
**sonner*** to ring
**sonnerie** *nf* (ringing of) bell
**sorcière** *nf* witch
**soudain** suddenly
**souris** *nf* mouse

**sous** *prep* under
**soutien-gorge** *nm* bra
**souvenir** *nm* souvenir; memory
**souvent** often
**spacieux, spacieuse** *adj* spacious
**spécialisé(e)** *adj* specialised
**spécialité** *nf* specialty
**sport** *nm* sport
**sportif, sportive** *adj* sporty
**stade** *nm* stadium
**stationné(e)** *adj* parked
**statue** *nf* statue
**stylo** *nm* pen
**sucre** *nm* sugar
**sujet** *nm* topic
**super** *adj inv* super
**superbe** *adj* brilliant, superb
**supermarché** *nm* supermarket
**sur** *prep* on
**surface** *nf* surface area
**surligneur** *nm* highlighter
**surprise** *nf* surprise
**survêtement** *nm* tracksuit
**suspect** *nm*, **suspecte** *nf* suspect
**symbole** *nm* symbol
**sympa** *adj inv fam* nice; friendly
**symphonie** *nf* symphony
**synthétique** *nm* synthetic

# T

**ta** *see* **ton**
**table** *nf* table
**tableau des trains au départ** *m* train departure board
**taille** *nf* size, build
  **de taille moyenne** average size
**tante** *nf* aunt
**tard** late
  **plus tard** later
**tarte** *nf* tart
**tasse** *nf* cup
**tatie** *nf fam* auntie
**taxe** *nf* tax
**techno(logie)** *nf* technology
**tee-shirt** *nm* T-shirt
**télé(vision)** *nf* television
**téléphone** *nm* telephone
**téléphoner*** *v* to telephone
**température** *nf* temperature

**temps** *nm* weather; time
  **quel temps fait-il ?**
    what's the weather like?
**tennis** *nm* tennis
**terminer*** *v* to finish
**terrain** *nm* **de jeu** playing
  field
**terrasse** *nf* terrace
**terrible** *adj* terrible
**tes** *see* **ton**
**tête** *nf* head
**thé** *nm* tea
**théâtre** *nm* theatre
**timide** *adj* shy
**tirer*** *v* to pull
**toi** you
**toilettes** *nfpl* toilet
**tomate** *nf* tomato
**tomber*** *v* to fall
**ton, ta, tes** your
**tonton** *nm fam* uncle
**tortue** *nf* tortoise
**tôt** early
**toujours** always
**tournée** *nf* round
**tourner*** *v* to turn
**tout, toute, tous, toutes** all
  **tous les deux** both
  **tous les jours** everyday
  **tout droit** straight ahead
  **tout le monde** everyone
  **tout près (de)** very near
  **tout(e) seul(e)** by one's
  self, on one's own

**traditionnel(le)** *adj*
  traditional
**train** *nm* train
**traîneau** *nm* sled, sleigh
**travail** *nm* job, work
**travailler*** *v* to work
**traverser*** *v* to cross
**trente** thirty
**très** very
  **très bien** very well
**tribu** *nf* tribe
**trois** three
**trop** too; too much
  **c'est trop fort, ça !** *fam*
  that's pushing it!
**tropiques** *nmpl* tropics
  **sous les tropiques** in the
  tropics
**trottoir** *nm* footpath
**trousse** *nf* pencil case
**tu** you
**typique** *adj* typical

# U V

**un, une** one; a
**utile** *adj* useful
**va** *see* **aller**
**vacances** *nfpl* holidays
**vachement** *fam* really, so
**vaisselle** *nf* dishes, washing
  up
**vanille** *nf* vanilla
**vaste** *adj* huge

**végétarien(ne)** *adj*
  vegetarian
**vélo** *nm* bicycle
**vendre*** *v* to sell
  **à vendre** for sale
**vendredi** *nm* Friday
**venir** *v* to come
**vent** *nm* wind
  **il y a du vent** it is windy
**verbe** *nm* verb
**vérifier*** *v* to check
**verre** *nm* glass
**vers** *prep* towards
**vert(e)** *adj* green
**vêtements** *nmpl* clothes
tu **veux** you want
**viande** *nf* meat
**vieux (vieil), vieille** *adj* old
  **le vieux Québec** old
  Quebec
**ville** *nf* city, town
  **centre ville** city centre,
  town centre
  **en ville** in the city/town
**visible** *adj* visible
**violet(te)** *adj* purple
**visiter*** *v* to visit
**vite** quickly
**vocabulaire** *nm* vocabulary
**voici** here is, here are
**voie** *nf* platform, track
**voilà** there is, there are,
  there you are
**voile** *nf* sail; sailing

**voisin** *nm*, **voisine** *nf*
  neighbour
**voisinage** *nm*
  neighbourhood
**voiture** *nf* car; carriage
**voix** *nf* voice
**vol** *nm* flight
**votre, vos** your
je **voudrais ...** I would
  like ...
vous **voulez ...?**
  do you want ...?
**vous** you
**voyager**** *v* to travel
**voyons ...** let's see ...
**vrai(e)** *adj* true, real
**vraiment** really
**VTT (vélo tout terrain)** *nm*
  mountain bike
**vue** *nf* view

# W X Y Z

**week-end** *nm* weekend
**yeux** *nmpl* eyes
**zut !** *fam* darn!, damn!

*n* = noun  *m* = masculine  *f* = feminine  *pl* = plural  *v* = verb  *prep* = preposition  *adj* = adjective  *inv* = invariable  *fam* = familiar

\* = regular verb (see page 50)    \*\* = semi-regular –er verb (see page 51)    ❖ = irregular verb (see page 51)

# A

**a, an** un, une
to **accompany** *v* accompagner\*
**address** *n* adresse *f*
**aerobics** *n* aérobique *f*
**aeroplane** *n* avion *m*
  **by aeroplane** en avion
**Africa** *n* Afrique *f*
**after** après *f*
  **afternoon** *n* après-midi *m*
  **this afternoon** cet après-midi
**again** encore
**ages** *n* éternité *f*
  **we've been waiting for ages!** ça fait une éternité qu'on attend !
to **agree** *v* être❖ d'accord
**air** *n* air *m*
**airport** *n* aéroport *m*
**aisle seat** *n* place *f* côté couloir
**alone** *adj* seul(e)
**along** *prep* le long de
**already** déjà
**also** aussi
**always** toujours
**and** et
**animal** *n* animal *m*, animaux *pl*
**answer** *n* réponse *f*
to **answer** *v* répondre\*
**apartment** *n* appartement *m*
to **apologise** *v* s'excuser\*
**apple** *n* pomme *f*
**apricot** *n* abricot *m*
**Arabic (language)** *n* arabe *m*
**arcade (video games)** *n* salle *f* de jeux
**archery** *n* tir *m* à l'arc
to **argue** *v* se disputer\*
to **arrive** *v* arriver\*
**art** *n* dessin *m*
**as … as** aussi … que
  **as tall as** aussi grand que
to **ask a question** *v* poser\* une question

**asparagus** *n* asperges *fpl*
**athletics** *n* athlétisme *m*
**attack** *n* attaque *f*
  to **attack** *v* attaquer\*
**aunt** *nf* tante
  **auntie** *n* tatie *f*
**Australia** *n* Australie *f*
**Australian** *n* Australien *m*, Australienne *f* ♦ *adj* australien(ne)
**average size** de taille moyenne
**avocado** *n* avocat *m*

# B

**back-to-school** *n* rentrée *f*
**bad** *adj* mauvais(e)
  **badly** mal
  **not bad** pas mal
**badminton** *n* badminton *m*
**bag** *n* sac *m*
**baggage** *n* bagage *m*
**baker** *n* boulanger *m*, boulangère *f*
**bakery** *n* boulangerie *f*
**balcony** *n* balcon *m*
**bald** *adj* chauve
**ball** *n* ballon *m*
**banana** *n* banane *f*
**bank** *n* banque *f*
**baseball** *n* base-ball *m*
**basketball** *n* basket(-ball) *m*
**bathers** *n* maillot *m* de bain
**bathroom** *n* salle *f* de bain
to **be** *v* être❖
**beach** *n* plage *f*
**bean (green)** *n* haricot *m* vert
**beard** *n* barbe *f*
**beautiful** *adj* beau (bel), belle
**because** parce que
**bed** *n* lit *m*
  **to make the bed** *v* faire le lit
**bedroom** *n* chambre *f*
**bedspread** *n* couvre-lit *m*
**beer** *n* bière *f*

**beetroot** *n* betterave *f*
**before** *prep* avant
to **begin** *v* commencer\*\*
**behind** *prep* derrière
I don't **believe you!** mon œil !
(ringing of) **bell** *n* sonnerie *f*
**belt** *n* ceinture *f*
**beside** *prep* à côté (de)
**big** *adj* grand(e), gros(se)
**bike** *n* vélo *m*
  **to go bike riding** *v* faire du vélo
  **mountain bike** VTT (vélo tout terrain)
**bill** *n* addition *f*
**bird** *n* oiseau *m*, oiseaux *pl*
**birthday** *n* anniversaire *m*
**biscuit** *n* biscuit *m*
**blackboard** *n* tableau *m* noir
**blonde** *adj* blond(e)
to **blush** *v* rougir\*
**book** *n* livre *m*
**bookcase** *n* bibliothèque *f*
**boot** *n* botte *f*
**boring** *adj* rasant(e) *fam*, ennuyeux, ennuyeuse
**both** tous les deux
**bowls** *n* boules *fpl*
**boxer shorts** *n* caleçon *m*
**boxing** *n* boxe *f*
**boy** *n* garçon *m*
**bra** *n* soutien-gorge *m*
**bracelet** *n* bracelet *m*
**bread** *n* pain *m*
  **breadstick** *n* baguette *f* (de pain)
to **break** *v* casser\*
**breakfast** *n* petit-déjeuner *m*
you're a **bright one!** gros malin ! *fam*
**brooch** *n* broche *f*
**brother** *n* frère *m*
**brown** *adj* brun(e) (*hair, etc.*), marron *inv* (*clothes, eyes etc.*)
  **chestnut brown** *adj* châtain(e) *m*

**Brussels sprouts** *n* choux *mpl* de Bruxelles
**bus** *n* bus *m*
  **by bus** en bus *m*
  **bus station** *n* gare *f* des autobus
**bushwalking** *n* randonnée *f*
  **to go bushwalking** *v* faire de la randonnée
**but** mais
**butter** *n* beurre *m*
to **buy** *v* acheter\*\*

# C

**cabbage** *n* chou *m*
**café** *n* café *m*
**cake** *n* gâteau *m*; pâtisserie *f*
**calm down!** du calme !
**canteen** *n* cantine *f*
**cap** *n* casquette *f*
**capsicum** *n* poivron *m*
**car** *n* voiture *f*
**card** *n* carte *f*
**carriage** *n* voiture *f*
**carrot** *n* carotte *f*
to **carry** *v* porter\*
**castle** *n* château *m*
**cat** *n* chat *m*
**cathedral** *n* cathédrale *f*
to **celebrate** *v* fêter\*
**celery** *n* céleri *m*
**cellar** *n* cave *f*
**central bus station** *n* gare *f* des autobus
**chair** *n* chaise *f*
to **change** *v* changer\*\*
to **check** *v* vérifier\*
**cheer up!** courage !
**cheese** *n* fromage *m*
  **cheese shop** *n* fromagerie
**chemist** *n* pharmacie *f*
**chicken** *n* poulet *m*
**child** *n* enfant *mf*
**Chinese (language)** *n* chinois *m*
**chips (crisps)** *n* chips *fpl*
**chips (fries)** *n* frites *fpl*

**chocolate** n chocolat m
**chocolate mousse** n
   mousse f au chocolat
to **choose** v choisir*
**church** n église f
**cinema** n ciné(ma) m
**citadel** n citadelle f
**city** n ville f
   **city centre** centre ville m
   **in the city** en ville
**class** n classe f
**classical music** n musique f
   classique
to **close** v fermer*
**clothes** n vêtements mpl
**coat** n manteau m,
   manteaux pl
**Coca-Cola** n coca(-cola) m
**cockatoo** n cacatoès m
**coconut** n noix f de coco
**coffee** n café m
   **coffee with milk** n
   café au lait
**cold** adj froid(e)
   **it is cold** il fait froid
**colour** n couleur f
to **come** v venir
   **come on (the) … !**
   allez (les) … !
   **I'm coming** j'arrive
**competition** n
   compétition f
**computer studies** n
   informatique f
**conductor** n contrôleur m
to **congratulate** v féliciter*
to **confuse** v confondre*
**congratulations!**
   félicitations !
to **continue** v continuer*
to do the **cooking** v faire✷
   la cuisine
**cool** adj inv fam cool;
   adj frais m, fraîche f
**corn** n maïs m
to **correspond (with)** v
   correspondre* (avec)
**costume** n costume m
**couch** n canapé m
**country** n pays m
**cousin** n cousin m,
   cousine f
**crazy** adj fam dingue
**crew cut** adj cheveux en
   brosse
**cricket** n cricket m
**croissant** n croissant m
   **ham croissant** croissant
   au jambon
to **cross** v traverser*

**cucumber** n concombre m
**cup** n tasse f
**curly** adj frisé(e)
**customer** n client m,
   cliente f
**cute** adj mignon(ne)
to go **cycling** v faire✷ du
   velo / du cyclisme

# D

**dad** n papa m
**dairy (NZ)** n épicerie f
**damn!** mince ! fam, zut ! fam
to **dance** v danser*
**dangerous** adj dangereux,
   dangereuse
**dark** adj foncé(e)
**daughter** n fille f
**day** n jour m, journée f
**dear** adj cher, chère
to **decide** v décider*
**degree** n degré m
   **it is … degree(s)**
   il fait … degré(s)
**delicious** adj délicieux,
   délicieuse
**departure** n départ m
   **train departure board**
   tableau des trains au
   départ
**desk** n bureau m
**dessert** n dessert m
**difficult** adj difficile
to **dine (evening meal)** v
   dîner*
**discount shop, market** n
   braderie f
**disgusting** adj dégoûtant(e)
**dish** n plat m
   **to do the dishes** v
   faire la vaisselle
to **do** v faire✷
**dog** n chien m
**door** n porte f
**drama** n art m dramatique
to **draw** v dessiner*
**drawing** n dessin m
you're **dreaming!** tu planes !
**dress** n robe f
   **to get dressed** v
   s'habiller*
**dressing table** n coiffeuse f
**drink** n boisson f
to **drink** v boire
**driver** n conducteur m,
   conductrice f
**during** prep pendant

# E

**early** adj tôt
**earring** n boucle f d'oreille
**east** n est m
**easy** adj facile
to **eat** v manger**
**eggplant** n aubergine f
**eh?** hein ?
**elegant** adj élégant(e)
**email** n e-mail m
to **end** v terminer*, finir*
**English (language)** n
   anglais m
**enjoy your meal!** bon
   appétit !
**enough** assez
**entrance** n entrée f
**eraser** n gomme f
**error** n erreur f
**euro (European Union**
   **currency)** n euro m
**even** même
**evening** n soir m
**exchange** n échange m
   **student exchange** n
   échange scolaire
to **excuse oneself**
   v s'excuser*
   **excuse me** excusez-moi
**exercise book** n cahier m
**expensive** adj cher, chère
**eye** n œil m, yeux pl

# F

**facing** en face (de)
**fair** adj juste
   **it is not fair!** ce n'est
   pas juste !
to **fall** v tomber*
**family** n famille f
   **family name** n nom m
   de famille
   **family room** n salle f
   de séjour
   **host family** n famille f
   d'accueil
**fantastic** adj chouette fam,
   formidable fam, génial(e)
   fam, super fam inv, extra
   fam inv
**far** adj loin
   **far from** prep loin de
**fast** adj rapide
**fat** adj gros(se), gras(se)
**father** n père m
**favourite** adj préféré(e)
I am **fed up** j'en ai marre
   fam

**fencing** n escrime f
   **to do fencing** v faire de
   l'escrime
**ferocious** adj féroce
to **fill** v remplir*
**film** n film m
**finally** finalement
**finish** n fin f
to **finish** v terminer*, finir*
**first** adj premier, première
   **first class** première classe
**fish** n poisson m
**fit** adj en bonne forme
**flight** n vol m
**flip-flops** n claquettes fpl
**floor (storey)** n étage m
**flower** n fleur f
to **fly** v voler*
it is **foggy** il y a du brouillard
**football (soccer)** n
   foot(ball) m
**for** pour
to **forget** v oublier*
**fork** n fourchette f
**French (language)** n
   français m
**fresh** adj frais, fraîche
**friend** n ami m, amie f,
   copain m, copine f
**friendly** adj sympa fam inv
**from … to …** de … à …
in **front (of)** prep devant
**fruit** n fruit m
   **dried fruit** n fruit m sec
   **fruit salad** n salade f
   de fruits
**fun** adj amusant(e)
   **to have fun** v s'amuser*
**funny** adj marrant(e),
   amusant(e)

# G

**games arcade** n salle f
   de jeux
**garage** n garage m
**garden** n jardin m
**gate** n porte f
**geography** n géo(graphie) f
**German (language)** n
   allemand m
to **get out of (a vehicle)** v
   descendre* de
to **get on/in** v monter*
   (dans)
**ghost** n fantôme m
**girl** n fille f
to **give** v donner*
to **give back** v rendre*
**glass** n verre m

**glasses** n lunettes fpl
**glove** n gant m
**gluestick** n bâton m de colle
to **go** v aller✣
  **go away!** va-t-en !
  **I'm going** j'y vais
  **let's go!** on y va !
to **go down** v descendre*
to **go up (a street)** v remonter* (une rue)
**goal** n but m
**goatee** n bouc m
**golf** n golf m
**good** adj bon(ne)
  **good evening** bonsoir
  **good luck!** bonne chance !
  **good night** bonne nuit
  **goodbye** au revoir
**gorgeous** adj mignon(ne), adorable
**grandfather** n grand-père m
  **grandpa** n fam papi m
**grandmother** n grand-mère f
  **grandma** n fam mamie f
**grandparents** n grands-parents mpl
**grape** n raisin m
**grapefruit** n pamplemousse m
**great** adj génial(e) fam, formidable fam, chouette fam, super fam inv, cool fam inv, extra fam inv
**greedy guts** n goinfre m fam
**Greek (language)** n grec m
**green** adj vert(e)
to **grow** v grandir*
to **grow up** v grandir*
to **guess** v deviner*
  **guess what!** devinez !
**gym** n gymnase m
**gymnastics** n gymnastique f
  **to do gymnastics** v faire de la gymnastique

**H**

**hair** n cheveux mpl
**ham** n jambon m
**handbag** n sac m à main
**happy** adj content(e), heureux, heureuse
**happy birthday!** bon anniversaire !
**harbour** n port m
**hat** n chapeau m

to **hate** v détester*
to **have** v avoir✣
  **to have fun** v s'amuser*
**hazel** adj inv noisette
**he** il
to **hear** v entendre*
**hello** bonjour; âllo (on the telephone)
to **help** v aider*
**her** son, sa, ses
**here** ici
  **here is, here are** voici
**hi!** salut !
**highlighter** n surligneur m
**hiking** n randonnée f
  **to go hiking** v faire de la randonnée
**hip hip hurrah!** hip hip hip hourra !
**his** son, sa, ses
**history** n histoire f
**hockey** n hockey m
**holidays** n vacances fpl
**homework** n devoirs mpl
to **hope** v espérer**
  **I hope so!** j'espère que oui !
**horrible** adj horrible
**horse** n cheval m, chevaux pl
  **to go horse-riding** v faire de l'équitation
**hospital** n hôpital m
**host family** n famille f d'accueil
**hot** adj chaud(e)
  **it is hot** il fait chaud
**hotel** n hôtel m
**hour** n heure f
**house** n maison f
**housework** n ménage m
  **to do the housework** v faire le ménage
**how** comment
  **how are you?** ça va ?
  **how do I get to ...?** pour aller à ... ?
  **how much is it?** c'est combien ?
**HSIE (subject)** n histoire-géo(graphie) f
**huge** adj énorme
**hunger** n faim f
  **to be hungry** v avoir faim
  **I am hungry** j'ai faim
to **hurry** v se dépêcher*
to be in a **hurry** être✣ v pressé(e)
**husband** n mari m

**I**

**I** je
**ice-cream** n glace f
**ice-hockey** n hockey m sur glâce
**ice-skating** n patinage m (sur glace)
  **to go ice-skating** v faire du patinage
  **ice-skating rink** n patinoire f
**if** si
**impatient** adj impatient(e)
**impossible** adj impossible
**in** prep dans
  **in Australia** en Australie f
  **in Canada** au Canada m
  **in the United States of America** aux Etats-Unis (d'Amérique) pl
  **in Quebec (city)** à Québec m
**Indonesian (language)** n indonésien m
**information technology** n techno(logie) f
**in-line skating** n roller m
  **to go in-line skating** v faire du roller
**intelligent** adj intelligent(e)
**interesting** adj intéressant(e)
**Internet café** n cybercafé m
to **introduce** v présenter*
**is** see **to be**
**Italian (language)** n italien m

**J**

**jacket** n blouson m
**jam** n confiture f
**jandal (NZ)** n claquette f
**Japanese (language)** n japonais m
**jeans** n jean m
**jersey** n pull(-over) m
**jet-ski** n jet-ski m
**job** n travail m
**judo** n judo m
**jumper** n pull(-over) m

**K L**

**karate** n karaté m
**kayak** n kayak m
  **to go kayaking** v faire du kayak
**kilo** n kilo m
**kiwi fruit** n kiwi m
**knickers** n slip m
**knife** n couteau m
**I know** je sais
  **I don't know** je ne sais pas
**lady** n dame f
**lamp** n lampe f
**language** n langue f
**large** adj gros(se)
**late** en retard
**Latin** n latin m
**laundry (room)** n buanderie f
**lazy** adj paresseux, paresseuse; fainéant(e) fam
to **learn** v apprendre✣
to **leave** v quitter*; partir
**left** n gauche f
  **to the left (of)** à gauche (de)
**lemon** n citron m
**lemonade** n limonade f
**less ... than** moins ... que
**lesson** n cours m
**lettuce** n salade m
**light (colour)** adj clair(e)
to **like** v aimer*
  **what is he/she like?** il/elle est comment ?
  **I would like ...** je voudrais ...
a **little** un peu
to **listen (to)** v écouter*
to **live** v habiter*
**lively** adj vif, vive
**living room** n salle f de séjour
**loaf (of bread)** n pain m
**lolly** n bonbon m
**long** adj long(ue)
to **look at** v regarder*
to **look for** v chercher*
to **look like** v ressembler*
to **lose** v perdre*
**lost** adj perdu(e)
**lots, a lot** beaucoup
**lounge** n salon m
to **love** v aimer*, adorer*
**lovely** adj beau (bel), belle
**luggage** n bagage m
**lunch** n déjeuner m
to have **lunch** v déjeuner*

# M

**magnificent** *adj* magnifique
to **make** *v* faire*
   **make yourself at home!** fais comme chez toi !
**man** *n* homme *m*
**mandarin** *n* mandarine *f*
**mango** *n* mangue *f*
**many** beaucoup (de)
**map** *n* carte *f*
   **town map** *n* plan *m* de la ville
**maple syrup** sirop *m* d'érable
**market** *n* marché *m*
   **discount market** *n* braderie *f*
**martial arts** *n* arts *mpl* martiaux
**mat** *n* tapis *m*
**match (sports)** *n* match *m*
**maths** *n* maths *fpl*
**mayonnaise** *n* mayonnaise *f*
**maybe** peut-être
**me** moi
   **me neither** moi non plus
   **me too** moi aussi
**meat** *n* viande *f*
to **meet (each other)** *v* (se) rencontrer*
**melon** *n* melon *m*
**menu** *n* carte *f*
**midday** *n* midi *m*
**mid-length** *adj* mi-long, mi-longue
**milk** *n* lait *m*
   **milk bar** *n* épicerie *f*
I don't **mind** ça m'est égal
**mineral water** *n* eau *f* minérale
**Miss** *n* Mademoiselle *f* (Mlle)
**mistake** *n* erreur *f*
**modern** *adj* moderne
**month** *n* mois *m*
**more** plus
**more ... than** plus ... que
**morning** *n* matin *m*
   **in the morning** du matin
**mother** *n* mère *f*
**mountain bike** *n* VTT (vélo *m* tout terrain)
   **to go mountain bike riding** *v* faire du VTT
**mouse** *n* souris *f*
**moustache** *n* moustache *f*
to **move** *v* bouger**
**Mr** *n* Monsieur *m* (M.)

**Mrs** *n* Madame *f* (Mme)
**much** beaucoup
**mum** *n* maman *f*
**museum** *n* musée *m*
**mushroom** *n* champignon *m*
**music** *n* musique *f*
**my** mon, ma, mes

# N

**name** *n* nom *m*
   **my name is** je m'appelle
   **first name** *n* prénom *m*
   **surname, family name** *n* nom de famille
**napkin** *n* serviette *f* (de table)
**nasty** *adj* méchant(e)
**naughty** *adj* méchant(e)
**navy (blue)** *adj* bleu marine *inv*
**near** *prep* près (de)
   **very near** tout près (de)
it is **necessary** il faut
**necklace** *n* collier *m*
**nectarine** *n* brugnon *m*
**neighbour** *n* voisin *m*, voisine *f*
the **Netherlands** *n* les Pays-Bas *mpl*
**new** *adj* nouveau (nouvel), nouvelle
**New Zealand** *n* Nouvelle-Zélande *f*
**news** *n* nouvelles *fpl*
**next to** *prep* à côté de
**nice** *adj inv* sympa *fam*, gentil(le)
   **it is nice weather** il fait beau
**nightie** *n* chemise *f* de nuit
**no** non
   **no way!** pas question !
**non-smoking** non-fumeur
**noon** *n* midi *m*
**north** *n* nord *m*
**not** ne ... pas
   **she is not looking** elle ne regarde pas
   **not at all** pas du tout
   **not bad** pas mal
   **not yet** pas encore
**now** maintenant
**number** *n* numéro *m*, nombre *m*

# O

**o'clock** *n* heure *f*
   **it is two o'clock** il est deux heures
**of** de, d'
**of course** bien sûr
**often** souvent
**OK** d'accord
**old** *adj* vieux (vieil), vieille
   **how old are you?** tu as quel âge ?
**on** *prep* sur
**one** un, une
   **one-way ticket** *n* aller simple *m*
**onion** *n* oignon *m*
**only** seulement
**open ...!** ouvrez ... !
**opposite** *prep* en face de
**or** ou
**orange** ♦ *adj* orange *inv*
   ♦ *n* orange *m*
   **orange juice** *n* jus *m* d'orange
**other** autre
**ouch!** aïe !
**our** notre, nos
**over there** là-bas

# P Q

**page** *n* page *f*
**pantyhose** *n* collant *m*
**parent** *n* parent *m*, parente *f*
**park** *n* parc *m*
**parsnip** *n* panais *m*
to **participate (in)** *v* participer* à
to **pass (by)** *v* passer*
**passenger** *n* passager *m*, passagère *f*
**pasta** *n* pâtes *fpl*
**patience** *n* patience *f*
**pawpaw** *n* papaye *f*
to **pay** *v* payer**
**peach** *n* pêche *f*
**pear** *n* poire *f*
**peas** *n* petits pois *mpl*
**pen** *n* stylo *m*
**pencil** *n* crayon *m*
**pencil case** *n* trousse *f*
**penfriend, penpal** *n* correspondant *m*, correspondante *f*
**perfect** *adj* parfait(e)
**perhaps** peut-être
**person** *n* personne *f*
**pet** *n* animal *m* familier

**pharmacy** *n* pharmacie *f*
**photo** *n* photo *f*
**physical education (PE)** *n* éducation *f* physique et sportive (EPS)
**physics** *n* physique *f*
**picture** *n* peinture *f*, tableau *m*
**pig (animal)** *n* cochon *m*
**pig (greedy guts)** *n* goinfre *m fam*
**pineapple** *n* ananas *m*
**pizza** *n* pizza *f*
**place** *n* place *f*
**plate** *n* assiette *f*
**platform** *n* voie *f*, quai *m*
to **play** *v* jouer*
   **to play tennis** *v* jouer au tennis
**player** *n* joueur *m*, joueuse *f*
**playing field** *n* terrain *m* de jeu
**please** s'il te plaît, s'il vous plaît
**police station** *n* poste *m* de police *m*, commissariat *m*, gendarmerie *f*
**poor** *adj* pauvre
**port** *n* port *m*
**possible** *adj* possible
**post office** *n* poste *f*
**postcard** *n* carte *f* postale
**poster** *n* poster *m*
**postie** *n* facteur *m*
**potato** *n* pomme *f* de terre
to **prefer** *v* préférer**
to **prepare** *v* préparer*
**pretty** *adj* joli(e)
**price** *n* prix *m*
**pumpkin** *n* citrouille *f*
**purple** *adj* violet(te)
**pyjamas** *n* pyjama *m*
a **quarter** *n* quart *m*
**question** *n* question *f*
**quick, quickly** vite

# R

**radish** *n* radis *m*
**raincoat** *n* imper(méable) *m*
it is **raining** il pleut
**raspberry** *n* framboise *f*
**rather** assez
to **read** *v* lire
**really** vraiment
   **really?** vraiment ?, ah bon ?
**recess** *n* récré(ation) *f*

**red-haired** *adj* roux, rousse
**referee** *n* arbitre *m*
**religious eduction (RE)** *n* éducation *f* religieuse
to **rent** *v* louer*
　**for rent** à louer
to **repeat** *v* répéter**
　**could you repeat that for me please?** vous voulez répéter, s'il vous plaît ?
to **resemble** *v* ressembler* à
to **reserve** *v* réserver*
**restaurant** *n* restaurant *m*
to **return** *v* retourner*
**return ticket** *n* aller-retour *m*
**rice** *n* riz *m*
**right** *n* droite *f*
　**to the right (of)** à droite (de)
　**that's right** c'est ça
to **ring** *v* téléphoner*
**ring binder** *n* classeur *m*
**rock (music)** *n* rock *m*
**room** *n* salle *f*
　**family room** salle de séjour
　**living room** salle de séjour
　**lounge room** *n* salon *m*
to do **rowing** *v* faire❖ de l'aviron
**rugby** *n* rugby *m*
**ruler** *n* règle *f*
**rumpsteak** *n* rumsteak *m*

# S

**sail** *n* voile *f*
　**to go sailing** *v* faire de la voile
**salad** *n* salade *f*
**salmon** *n* saumon *m*
　**smoked salmon** *n* saumon fumé
it's all the **same to me** ça m'est égal
**sandal** *n* sandale *f*
**sandwich** *n* sandwich *m*
　**cheese sandwich** sandwich au fromage
**scarf** *n* écharpe *f*
**school** *n* école *f*
　**junior secondary school (11–15 year olds)** *n* collège *m*
　**senior secondary school (15–18 year olds)** *n* lycée *m*

**science (biology)** *n* sciences *fpl* naturelles
**science (chemistry and physics)** *n* sciences *fpl* physiques
**scuba-diving** *n* plongée *f* sous-marine
　**to go scuba-diving** *v* faire de la plongée sous-marine
to **sculpt** *v* sculpter*
**seat** *n* place *f*
　**aisle seat** place côte couloir
　**window seat** place côté fenêtre
**second** *adj* deuxième
　**second class** deuxième classe
let's **see …** voyons …
**see you (later/soon)** à bientôt
to **seem** *v* sembler*
**self-service** *n* libre-service *m*
to **sell** *v* vendre*
　**for sale** à vendre
to **send** *v* envoyer**
**separated** *adj* séparé(e)
**serviette** *n* serviette *f* (de table)
to **settle in** *v* s'installer*
**severe** *adj* sévère
**she** elle
**sheet** *n* drap *m*
**shirt** *n* chemise *f*
**shoe** *n* chaussure *f*
**shop** *n* magasin *m*, boutique *f*
　**to do the shopping** *v* faire les courses
　**to go shopping** *v* faire du shopping
**short** *adj* court(e)
**shorts** *n* short *m*
**shy** *adj* timide
**silence** *n* silence *m*
**singlet top** *n* débardeur *m*
**sister** *n* sœur *f*
**sixth** *adj* sixième
**size** *n* taille *f*
in-line **skating** *n* roller *m*
　**to go in-line skating** *v* faire du roller (en ligne)
**skateboard** *n* skate *m*
　**to go skateboarding** *v* faire du skate
**skiing** *n* ski *m*
　**to go skiing** *v* faire du ski

**skinny** *adj* maigre
**skirt** *n* jupe *f*
**slack** *adj* fainéant(e) *fam*
to **sleep** *v* dormir
**slice** *n* tranche *f*
**slim** *adj* mince
**small** *adj* petit(e)
**small business** *n* petit commerce *m*
**smoking** fumeur
**snow** *n* neige *f*
　**it is snowing** il neige
**snowboard** *n* surf *m* des neiges
　**to go snowboarding** *v* faire du surf sur neige
**snowpea** *n* mange-tout *m*
**so** vraiment; alors
　**so-so** comme ci comme ça
　**so?, so what?** et alors ?
**social studies (subject)** *n* histoire-géo(graphie) *f*
**sock** *n* chaussette *f*
**sofa** *n* canapé *m*
**some** des
**someone** quelqu'un
**sometimes** quelquefois
**son** *n* fils *m*
**soon** bientôt
**sorry** désolé(e), pardon
　**I'm sorry** je suis désolé(e)
**SOSE (subject)** *n* histoire-géo(graphie) *f*
**spacious** *adj* spacieux, spacieuse
**Spanish (language)** *n* espagnol *m*
to **speak** *v* parler*
to **spend (time)** *v* passer*
**spiky (hair)** *adj* (les cheveux) en brosse
**spinach** *n* épinards *mpl*
**spoon** *n* cuillère *f*
**sport** *n* sport *m*
　**to do sport** *v* faire du sport
**sports shoes** *n* baskets *mpl*
**sporty** *adj* sportif, sportive
**squash** *n* squash *m*
**stadium** *n* stade *m*
**staircase, stairs** *n* escalier *m*
**station** *n* gare *f*
　**bus station** gare des autobus
**statue** *n* statue *f*
to **stay** *v* rester*
**still** encore
**stockings** *n* collant *m*

**storeroom** *n* cellier *m*
**storey** *n* étage *m*
**stadium** *n* stade *f*
**stationery shop** *n* papeterie *f*
**straight (hair)** *adj* (les cheveux) raide(s)
**straight ahead** tout droit
**strawberry** *n* fraise *f*
**stray** *adj* perdu(e)
**street** *n* rue *f*
**strict** *adj* sévère
**study** *n* bureau *m*
**stylish** *adj* chic *inv*
**subject (school)** *n* matière *f*
**subject (topic)** *n* sujet *m*
**sugar** *n* sucre *m*
**sun** *n* soleil *m*
　**sunglasses** *n* lunettes *fpl* de soleil
　**it is sunny** il y a du soleil
**supermarket** *n* supermarché *m*
to **surf** *v* surfer*
**surname** *n* nom *m* de famille
**surprise** *n* surprise *f*
**sweet** *n* bonbon *m*
**swimming** *n* natation *f*
　**to go swimming** *v* faire de la natation
**swimming pool** *n* piscine *f*
**swimsuit** *n* maillot *m* de bain

# T

**T-shirt** *n* tee-shirt *m*
**table** *n* table *f*
**table tennis** *n* tennis *m* de table, ping-pong *m*
to **take** *v* prendre❖
to **take part (in)** *v* participer* (à)
**tall** *adj* grand(e)
**tank top** *n* débardeur *m*
**tart** *n* tarte *f*
**tea** *n* thé *m*
**teacher** *n* prof(esseur) *mf*
**team** *n* équipe *f*
**technology** *n* technologie *f*
**telephone** *n* téléphone *m*
　**telephone number** *n* numéro *m* de téléphone
**tennis** *n* tennis *m*
**terrace** *n* terrasse *f*
**Thai-box** *n* boxe *f* thaï(landaise)
**thank you** merci

**that** ça
- **that makes** ça fait
- **that suits you!** ça te va bien !
- **that's all** c'est tout
- **that's it !** c'est ça !

**that** ce (cet), cette
**the** l', le, la, les
**theatre** n théâtre m
**their** leur, leurs
**then** alors; puis
**there** là
- **there is, there are, there you are** voilà
- **there is, there are** il y a

**these** ces
**they** ils, elles
**thin** adj maigre, mince
to **think** v penser*
**third** adj troisième
to be **thirsty** v avoir⁕ soif
- **I am thirsty** j'ai soif

**this** ce (cet), cette
**those** ces
**ticket** n billet m
- **one-way ticket** n aller simple m
- **return ticket** n aller-retour m
- **ticket machine** n billeterie f automatique
- **ticket office** n guichet m

to **tidy** v ranger**
**tie** n cravate f
**tights** n collant m
**time** n temps m, heure f
- **what time is it?** il est quelle heure?

**tiring** adj fatigant(e)
**today** aujourd'hui
**together** ensemble
**togs** n maillot m de bain
**toilet** n toilettes fpl
**tomato** n tomate f
**tomorrow** demain
- **see you tomorrow** à demain

**too** trop, aussi
- **too much** trop

**tourist office** n office m du tourisme
**towards** prep vers
**towel** n serviette f (de bain)
**town** n ville f
- **town hall** n hôtel m de ville
- **town map** n plan m de la ville
- **town square** n place f

**tracksuit** n survêtement m
**traditional** adj traditionnel(le)
**traffic light** n feu m, feux pl
**train** n train m
- **by train** en train
- **train station** n gare f

**tramping** n randonnée f
- **to go tramping** faire v de la randonnée

to **travel** v voyager**
**trousers** n pantalon m
**true** adj vrai(e)
**tuck shop** n cantine f
**tuna** n thon m
to **turn** v tourner*
**TV** n fam télé f
**twenty** vingt
**twin** n jumeau m, jumelle f, jumeaux mpl

# U V

**ugly** adj moche fam, laid(e)
**umpire** n arbitre m
**uncle** n oncle m
**under** prep sous
**underpants** n slip m
to **understand** v comprendre⁕
to get **undressed** v se déshabiller*
the **United States (of America)** n les États-Unis mpl (d'Amérique)
as **usual** comme d'habitude
**usually** d'habitude
**vacuum cleaner** n aspirateur m
- **to do the vacuuming** passer* l'aspirateur

to **validate (ticket)** v composter*
**vanilla** n vanille f
**vegetable** n légume m
**vegetarian** adj végétarien(ne)
**verb** n verbe m
**verify** v vérifier*
**very** très
**vet** n vétérinaire mf
**video shop** n vidéothèque f
**Vietnamese (language)** n vietnamien m
**Vietnamese (person)** adj vietnamien(ne)

**view** n vue f
to **visit** v visiter*
**village** n village m
**vocabulary** n vocabulaire m
**volleyball** n volley(-ball) m

# W

**waffle** n gaufre f
to **wait for** v attendre*
**waiter** n serveur m
**waitress** n serveuse f
**waiting room** n salle f d'attente
to **wake up** v se réveiller*
to go for a **walk** v faire⁕ une promenade
**wall** n mur m
you **want** tu veux, vous voulez
**wardrobe** n armoire f
to **wash** v laver*
- **to wash oneself** v se laver*

**wash house** n buanderie f
**watch** n montre f
to **watch** v regarder*
- **watch out for** attention à …

**water** n eau f
**waterskiing** n ski nautique m
- **to go waterskiing** v faire du ski nautique

**wavy** adj ondulé(e)
to **wear** v porter*
**weather** n temps m
- **it is nice weather** il fait beau

**week** n semaine f
**weekend** n week-end m
- **to spend the weekend** v passer le week-end

**weird** adj bizarre
you're **welcome** je vous en prie
**well** bien; alors, ben fam
- **well done!** bravo !

**what** quel, quelle, quels, quelles
- **what a surprise!** quelle surprise !
- **what is the weather like?** quel temps fait-il ?
- **what time is it?** il est quelle heure ?
- **what's that?** qu'est-ce que c'est ?

**when** quand
**where** où

**which** quel, quelle, quels, quelles
**who** qui
- **who is it? who's that?** qui est-ce ?
- **whose, to whom** à qui

**wholemeal bread** n pain m complet
**why** pourquoi
**wife** n femme f
to **win** v gagner*
**wind** n vent m
- **it is windy** il y a du vent

**window** n fenêtre f
- **window seat** n place f côté fenêtre

**windsurfing** n planche f à voile
- **to go windsurfing** v faire de la planche à voile

**wine** n vin m
**witch** n sorcière f
**with** avec
- **with pleasure** avec plaisir

**woman** n femme f
to **wonder** v se demander*
**wonderful** adj superbe
**work** n travail m
to **work** v travailler*
**I would like …** je voudrais …
to **write** v écrire
- **to write to** v correspondre* avec

# X Y Z

**year** n an m, année f
- **I'm twelve years old** j'ai douze ans

**yes** oui, si
**yogurt** n yaourt m
**you** tu; toi; vous
- **and you?** et toi ?, et vous ?

**young** adj jeune
**young people** n les jeunes mfpl
**your** ton, ta, tes; votre, vos
**yuk!** pouah !
**yum!** miam !
**zucchini** n courgette f

# Contents

# Acknowledgements

The authors would like to thank all the participants of the study who generously allowed us to interview them and to record their interviews. In particular, we would like to thank those participants who took part in focus group discussions at the initial and final stages of the research, and whose views and experiences shaped the writing of this report. We would also like to thank all the representatives of counselling agencies who took the time to cooperate with us in conducting the research. We would particularly like to express our appreciation to Saheliya in Edinburgh and EACH (Ethnic Alcohol Counselling in Hounslow) in London for facilitating access to their clients and for help in organising the focus group discussions.

We would also like to thank the members of our advisory group for their willingness in sharing their expertise with us and for the extremely supportive manner in which they did so: Shamshad Asqhar, Raspal Nottay, Nasa Begum, Simeela Khaliq, Valerie Graham, Rachel Milne, Ray de Souza, Professor S.P. Sashidharan, Dr Graham Foster, Colin Lee and Akin Fatunmbi.

Finally, we would like to thank the Joseph Rowntree Foundation for funding the project and Emma Stone, the project manager, for her valuable support throughout the research.

# Summary of findings

## Challenging myths and stereotypes about low take-up of counselling

| Myths and stereotypes | Our findings |
| --- | --- |
| Asian people are not interested in counselling | While non-clients have a low level of awareness of counselling, they are conscious of the limitations in the support available from family and friends. Once informed of the purpose of the service, the majority felt that it would be useful. Those who had experienced counselling and benefited from it expressed the need for the service to be publicised more widely in their communities. |
| Asian people do not use counselling services because language differences act as a barrier | Clients and non-clients vary in the extent to which they feel confident and comfortable speaking in English. For some Asian people, English would be their first choice. Others feel comfortable speaking in either English or an Asian language, while others would prefer speaking in an Asian language. |
| Asian people are not able to use a Western psychological model to work through their psychological distress | Clients show evidence of having used counselling sessions to confront difficult issues, work through their psychological difficulties and arrive at some means of dealing with their problems. Thus, the benefits which they are likely to gain are similar to that obtained by the majority population. |
| Counselling is only beneficial to white, middle-class people as it is derived from a Western tradition | The majority of clients benefited enormously from the experience of counselling. Some of the reported benefits were increased confidence and self-esteem, a greater sense of control over feelings and the ability to consider problems from a fresh perspective. |
| There is a high level of stigma associated with counselling in the Asian community | While a few clients express some fears about using counselling due to possible stigmatisation, these concerns do not appear to be so great as to prevent them from using the service. Clients and non-clients unanimously stress the importance of confidentiality in discussing personal details, and highly value this element of the service. |
| Asian people expect and need advice rather than counselling | Initially, most counselling clients (from the majority or minority ethnic population) are unclear about the purpose and nature of counselling, and may enter it with the expectation that they will be given advice. However, when familiar with the nature of the service, the qualities they value most are being 'heard' and treated with respect. |
| Asian people prefer to be directed either to black-led agencies or to Asian counsellors | Clients' preferences for counsellors are influenced by a number of factors. These include concerns about confidentiality, the ease with which they communicate in English and the extent to which they uphold cultural norms. Some clients strongly prefer a counsellor of the same ethnicity while others have a strong aversion to working with someone from the same ethnic background. Clients prefer to be consulted regarding the choice of counsellor, particularly when they are familiar with the service. Similarly, clients are also mixed in their preference for using either a mainstream or a black-led agency. |

# Counselling needs and preferences of Asian clients and non-clients compared with agency responses

|  | Client needs | Response of agencies |
|---|---|---|
| **Need for information** | Most non-clients expressed a desire to find out more about the nature and availability of counselling services. They preferred to be informed through personal contacts or outreach work. In contrast, clients were keen to have more information about the range of services available locally. | In contrast to black-led agencies which generally carried out considerable outreach work, there was little evidence that the majority of mainstream agencies invested effort in strategically targeting black communities when publicising their services. |
| **Right to be consulted and exercise choice** | Clients expressed a desire to be consulted concerning the nature of their therapy and their prospective counsellor's ethnicity and gender. They unanimously preferred to see a counsellor who was mature and experienced. Generally, female clients expressed a strong preference for working with female counsellors. | Agencies generally undertake an initial meeting to identify the client's needs and explain the nature of the service and the structure of the sessions. Counsellors are usually allocated on the basis of availability and/or their level of experience. If a preference is explicitly expressed, agencies generally attempt to meet it wherever possible. The shortage of black and male counsellors make it difficult to offer choice where these are specific requirements. In addition, clients may be faced with a trade-off between exercising choice and the length of time they would have to wait for counselling to begin. |
| **Preference for using a particular language** | Participants had a strong wish to be counselled in the language with which they were most comfortable. However, with some Asian language speakers, this preference was mitigated by a concern that the counsellor might be a member of their community. | Black-led agencies are usually able to offer counselling in a number of Asian languages as well as in English. A minority of agencies 'buy in' counsellors to meet specific language requirements. In contrast, most mainstream agencies generally assume that their clients are able and willing to communicate in English. Generally, the shortage of trained black counsellors limits agencies' ability to provide a choice of language. |
| **Choice of venue** | While clients were generally satisfied with receiving counselling at the venue provided, non-clients felt that they would like the option of being seen at home. | Agencies generally hold counselling sessions within their premises. In exceptional cases, some agencies will arrange for counsellors to meet clients in a more convenient alternative setting, including the home. |
| **Right to cultural sensitivity** | Both clients and non-clients expect counsellors to be interested in and respect their cultural values, religious beliefs and traditions, regardless of the counsellor's own cultural and religious background. | All agencies and counsellors emphasised their willingness and readiness to respect the cultural and religious beliefs of their clients, irrespective of whether or not they shared them. However, black-led agencies highlighted their ability to offer a service which is underpinned by an intimate knowledge of their clients' cultures. |

# Introduction

The most striking change in mental health policy in the United Kingdom in the last century has been the shift from institutional care to community-based services. These services include psychiatric services, counselling and psychotherapy, befriending schemes and drop-in facilities. Such services have a strong emphasis on supporting mental well-being and preventing its deterioration to the point where admission to hospital might become necessary. They also support the transition of those experiencing institutionalised care to life in the community. Among these services, counselling is one of the most widely available. It plays an important role in relieving psychological distress by allowing individuals the opportunity to articulate painful feelings and experiences, develop understanding and insight and make considered choices.

The mental health problems of black people have received considerable attention. However, as noted by Watters (1996), relatively little consideration has been given to black people's perceptions, needs and experiences of mental health services and the appropriateness of specific services, including counselling.

Several recent policy documents provide the opportunity to consider a new approach and framework for recognising the need for culturally sensitive mental health services for black people.

The Green Paper *Our healthier nation* (DoH, 1998) recognises inequalities in health among certain groups of people due to poverty, unemployment, bad housing and educational and environmental problems. This has particular implications for black people who have been shown to be disadvantaged in many of these areas. With specific reference to Scotland, the White Paper *Towards a healthier Scotland* (Scottish Executive, 1999) identifies mental health (along with cancer and coronary heart disease) as one of three leading priorities for the National Health Service (NHS). *The framework for mental health services in Scotland* (DoH, 1997) provides guidance for those charged with ensuring the development of comprehensive mental health services. Particular emphasis is given to improving working relationships between agencies, and to promoting greater understanding and coordinated responses to the mental health needs of vulnerable individuals and groups.

Recognition of the need for greater sensitivity to the circumstances of black people in planning community-based services is not new. Indeed, the government White Paper *Caring for people* (DoH, 1989) explicitly recognised that:

> ... people from different cultural backgrounds may have particular needs and problems.... Good community care will take account of the circumstances of minority communities and will be planned in consultation with them.

This study involves Asian people who have experienced psychological distress in considering their counselling needs. We examine the perceptions of those who have not been for counselling and consider the factors which might encourage them to use the service. We also examine the views of those who have been for counselling and consider the impact of the experience on their lives. On the basis of the needs and preferences that we have identified, we evaluate the accessibility and appropriateness of counselling provision in the voluntary sector for black people, in particular Asian people.

In this chapter, we will highlight the limitations of existing services in meeting the mental health needs of Asian people. We will discuss the failure of general practitioners (GPs) to recognise psychological difficulties within this group and hence refer them to appropriate services. We will also draw attention to the influence of socio-cultural factors in contributing to psychological distress. We will then consider Asian people's dissatisfaction with mental health services and their willingness to consider non-medical services. Finally, we will outline the aims of our research and explain its significance in the context of a growing user-led movement in mental health services.

## A note on definitions

The term 'Asian' is used to collectively describe those people who were born in Bangladesh, India and Pakistan and their descendants. We are aware that while this is a common means of grouping these people in the UK, not all the people to whom we apply this term identify themselves in this way or share a common culture. In the report, this recognition is reflected in the use of participants' own descriptions of their ethnicity, for example, Pakistani-Scottish or British-Indian.

The definition of counselling we have used in this study is closely aligned to that offered by the British Association for Counselling (BAC), a major professional body representing counselling in the UK:

> The purpose of counselling is to provide you with the opportunity to discuss your problems with a suitably qualified person. This person does not judge you, give you advice or talk about your situation to anyone else. He or she tries to understand your situation from your point of view and helps you to see yourself and your problems in a new light. This can help you to cope with problems better and bring about necessary changes in your life.

As is conventional in the counselling world, we refer to people who use counselling services as clients. People who have not used counselling services are referred to as non-clients.

## Relationships between mental health and ethnicity

Views on what constitutes normal and abnormal behaviour vary across cultures. Explanations of mental illness which attempt to account for why people fall ill and how they can most appropriately be treated are culture-bound. Kleinman (1977, p 4, cited in Fenton and Sadiq-Sangster,1996) has noted that:

> ... culture does considerably more than shape illness as an experience; it shapes the very way that we conceive of illness.

However, as Fenton and Sadiq-Sangster point out, very little attention has been paid to black people's own descriptions of illness, symptoms and causes of ill-health. Instead, research on the relationship between ethnicity and mental health in the UK has concentrated mainly on highlighting the differences in:

- the incidence of certain mental illnesses between minority ethnic groups;
- the routes by which people reach mental health services;
- cultural factors in the treatment of minority ethnic groups.

## Psychological distress in Asian people

A high prevalence of depression has been consistently noted among Asian people (Bhatnagar and Frank, 1997; Jacob et al, 1998; Odell et al, 1997; Silveira and Shah, 1998). Some of the particularly striking manifestations of psychological distress which have been identified are the higher rates of attempted suicide, deliberate self-harm and suicide among young Asian women (Ananthanarayanan, 1994; Prosser, 1996; Sheth et al, 1994). Among Indian men, a high rate of psychiatric admission has been noted in relation to alcohol dependence (Ananthanarayanan, 1994; McKeigue and Karmi, 1993).

Examining the factors which have contributed to psychological problems among Asian people, the recent explanations are socio-cultural rather than biological. Hatfield et al (1996) found that commonly cited stressors were lack of official support; crime and personal safety;

unemployment; financial problems and anxieties about children. Research conducted in Newcastle found that racism, fear of crime and racially-motivated crime were also high on the list of causes of mental health problems experienced by Asian respondents (Save the Children, 1997). In contrast, research carried out among Asian women in Glasgow (Tyrrell, 1998) showed that while respondents identified racism as one of the contributory factors, family problems, loneliness and bereavement were cited as the main sources of their depression, fear and stress.

Significantly, it has been found that the explanations of Asian people of the factors contributing to their mental health problems can differ significantly from those of practitioners. For example, in Tyrrell's study, respondents attached greater significance to external problems, such as employment, finance and racism, as sources of their mental distress. In contrast, practitioners perceived internal factors, mainly family problems, as the main cause of mental suffering experienced by Asian people.

## Lack of recognition of psychological problems by general practitioners

Research has shown that in many cases, GPs do not detect psychological problems in their Asian patients (Jacob et al, 1998; Lloyd, 1993; Odell et al, 1997). Since GPs are important 'gate-keepers' to specialist mental health services in the UK, their failure to diagnose mental health difficulties among Asian patients hinders their access to appropriate services.

Approaching the issue from a different perspective, Jacob et al (1998) have suggested that Asian people are less likely to perceive depression as an illness which requires medical treatment and, consequently, are less likely to disclose their psychological problems to their GP. This is supported by other studies which note that Asian women are particularly reluctant to seek help from GPs for depression or anxiety (Littlewood and Lipsedge, 1997; Save the Children, 1997).

Clearly, misdiagnosis and misinterpretation of behaviour are more likely to arise where cultural and language differences exist between patients and health professionals. However, it is important to recognise that language differences may be

given undue prominence in explaining the inability of GPs to detect psychological distress. Bowes and Domokos (1997) point out that this is only one barrier among many factors, such as the dearth of information, absence of cultural sensitivity and lack of local services in the area. They highlight that, in attempting to explain differential rates of service use between ethnic groups, attention should not be diverted from other important factors such as gender, race and class prejudice.

## Lack of appropriate forms of treatment

Where Asian people have succeeded in accessing mental health services, research has found a high level of dissatisfaction with these services. For example, Radia (1996) found that Asian users in certain London boroughs felt ignored by professionals and unhappy about being given medication rather than being listened to. Similarly, Hatfield et al's (1996) study on appropriate forms of treatment for mental illness for Asian people noted many critical comments about the value of electro-convulsive therapy and medication. In particular, it highlighted the need for 'someone to listen' and found 'almost universal support' for the provision of counselling and support to individuals experiencing mental health problems, and advice for their families.

The need for more preventive services such as counselling and for alternatives to medication is supported by Donaghy's (1997) research on depression in South Asian women. This study found that one of the key factors which increased the risk of depression was the absence of 'a strong confiding relationship'.

## The aims of this research

The main aims of our study were to:

- identify Asian people's perceptions and views of counselling;
- examine their experience of accessing and using counselling services;
- explore their preferences for the service;
- review the accessibility of service provision of voluntary agencies which provide counselling;
- examine the cultural sensitivity of counselling provision in voluntary sector agencies.

## Why the research is important

The research that we have cited reveals a number of compelling factors for considering better mental health services for Asian people, including:

- a high prevalence of depression;
- the influence of socio-cultural factors – including racism – in contributing to psychological distress;
- the lack of GPs' success in identifying psychological problems in this group and consequently their failure to refer individuals to appropriate services;
- Asian people's dissatisfaction with existing mental health services
- an openness on the part of Asian people to using non-medical forms of intervention, such as counselling;
- a low uptake of counselling services among Asian people.

It has been suggested that strong social and family networks among Asian people may delay the onset of mental illnesses such as schizophrenia (Burnett et al, 1999). While the existence of informal supportive relationships undoubtedly contributes to mental well-being, there is an extensive body of literature which reveals both the non-existence of the extended family and its limited ability to provide adequate support to its members (Netto, 1998; Walker, 1996). From a different perspective, the devastating impact on family members supporting a mentally ill person has also been recorded (Cuijpers, 1999).

It is not our view that counselling is the only means of supporting those experiencing mental health difficulties. However, the low take-up of such services by Asian people and other minority ethnic groups (Birmingham City Council, 1995) merits attention given the role of early intervention strategies in preventing the deterioration of mental ill health, and the rapid expansion of counselling service provision (Busfield,1999).

As has been frequently pointed out, the counselling services provided in the UK are derived from predominantly Western traditions. Thus, the relevance of generic counselling services to non-Western people cannot be assumed. There is growing awareness of issues of race, ethnicity and culture in the counselling profession, evidenced by the development of counselling practices such as 'transcultural counselling', 'multi-cultural counselling' and 'inter-cultural counselling' which explicitly seek to consider these issues (D'Ardenne and Mahatani, 1989; Moodley, 1999, 2000a, 2000b). Our research, however, is not concerned with examining the appropriateness of these theoretical models of counselling. Instead, we focus on the perceptions and experiences of clients and non-clients of counselling services, locating our study in the context of a growing user-led movement, motivated by recognition of:

- the right of users to better information, a choice of treatment and respect as individuals;
- the central importance of the views and perspectives of users of mental health services;
- the potential for and actual abuse of users of mental health services (Copperman and McNamara, 1999; Williams and Keating, 1999).

The research is also motivated by the recognition that, as user movements grow in strength, service providers are increasingly expected to take their views into account in the planning and delivery of services. With particular reference to counselling, the subjective, interpersonal nature of the service demands that clients' views on the impact of the service on themselves and their circumstances be placed centre-stage (Macran et al, 1999).

## The people and agencies in this study

The first part of the research is based on the views of 38 Asian people, 19 of whom had disclosed that they were experiencing anxiety, stress or depression and 19 of whom had used counselling services for a similar range of problems. Ranging in age from 21 to 75, the sample consisted of 15 men and 23 women. Most of the participants had migrated to the UK, with the number of years of residency in this country varying from three to 39 years. The overwhelming majority of participants were married with children. Most were able to speak an Asian community language as well as English, with differing levels of confidence and facility in both languages. Half of the participants were either in paid employment or were caring for the home and children. A quarter were unemployed, and the remainder were either students, retired or unable to work. Details of how the participants were identified and interviewed, and the ethical considerations which were observed, are given in

Appendix A. Their personal details are provided in Appendix B. All names have been changed in the report.

The second part of the study consists of a review of counselling service provision by 13 voluntary sector agencies. The rationale for selecting the agencies is given in Appendix A and the agencies are listed in Appendix C.

## Structure of the report

This introductory chapter is followed by four chapters of findings. Chapter 2 examines the extent of support which Asian clients and non-clients obtain from their families and friends and their perceptions of how this support differs from that offered by counselling. Chapter 3 considers the experiences of people who have accessed counselling, their views of the process and the impact of counselling on them. In Chapter 4 we discuss the preferences of both clients and non-clients of counselling with respect to important elements of the service. This is followed in Chapter 5 by a review of service provision by voluntary sector agencies. Finally, in Chapter 6, we draw together the findings from the previous chapters and highlight implications for policy and practice.

# 2

# Supportive relationships

The extent of informal support which individuals experience from family members and friends is likely to influence their views on the usefulness of counselling as a means of enabling them to cope with difficult personal circumstances. Drawing on the accounts of the clients and non-clients in the study, this chapter considers the extent of support which they experience from their families and friends. It also explores participants' views of the differences between this form of informal support and that which is likely to be obtained through counselling.

## Support from family and friends

Most participants had family in the UK and were either living with them, or close to them. In most cases, they could talk to and share personal problems with family members who would also confide in them. Contact was maintained on an almost daily basis and, generally, participants felt very comfortable in these relationships.

Some participants also reported that they had friends whom they could confide in and who would also confide in them. They generally met on a weekly or fortnightly basis. Participants differed in the extent to which they preferred confiding in either family or friends. They also made distinctions about what they would talk about to family members and friends. Below, Bushra (age 32) explains why she would rather confide in her friends:

> "My parents are there for me, but I find that I can't talk to them about really intimate things, I don't feel comfortable about telling them what's going on inside

my head. I'd rather speak to my friends about it." (Scottish-Asian)

Other participants reported that they were selective about which friends they talked to, and that their choice of confidant varied according to the nature of the topic they wanted to discuss.

## Issues of concern

It was clear that many participants often held back from entirely confiding in their family and friends. Issues of confidentiality and trust were often of considerable concern ("They would one thing to your face and another thing behind your back"). Others felt reluctant to disclose their concern over family members to friends for fear of losing respect within the community.

Many participants also felt restricted in what they could discuss with their immediate family, and this was sometimes related to a perception that they would not be understood. Other participants frequently reported how they could not discuss problems they were experiencing in relation to one member of the family with other members, because of the divided loyalties of the latter. This was particularly the case where there were intricate familial links, for example, in consanguineous marriages. Others felt that they simply could not discuss intimate issues with close family members.

Some participants felt that their family or friends were likely to attempt to influence their views or manipulate the situation. This was Shahida's experience when she found that her relationship with her husband was deteriorating:

"I wanted separation and they [her husband's family] were saying, 'Oh, try again, make the marriage work. You are two of the most wonderful people'."
(Indian)

Eventually, Shahida's inability to find sufficient support within her own network led her to seek professional help from a counselling service.

## Coping with change and managing feelings of distress

Non-clients spoke about a general sense of feeling lonely and alone with their problems. This was particularly true for recent migrants who found that people in the UK have a very different lifestyle:

"Everyone is busy, someone in their shop, someone elsewhere." (Sakhi, East African)

"Everything's strange in this country, the whole environment and living standards." (Aysha, Pakistani)

Other recurrent themes in the interviews were a sense of having to learn new 'rules' and a new 'way of living', and a sense of loss of the supportive network that they had been accustomed to in their country of origin. Some people were struggling to adapt to life in the UK as well as coping with other significant changes, as was the case for Aysha who had migrated to the UK soon after her marriage:

"I got married and came to this country ... and then my son was born, it's a very big change, I became a mother, and I've lost friends and family". (Pakistani)

A number of participants were coping with either physical ill-health or depression. Others were coping with the illness or death of close relatives. Yet others were concerned about their adult children who were not conforming to traditional expectations. Suki, born in the UK 50 years ago, was extremely distressed when her son broke off his wedding engagement and left the family home:

"We had to let him do what he wanted to do, which [was] he wanted to move out, so that was a major thing and it really

upset me, and really hurt me, and I still don't think I've got over it. I don't think I'll get over it until he comes back home." (Scottish-Sikh)

A few participants were struggling with severe financial difficulties and a lack of knowledge of how to access available forms of practical support. In the words of Banoo, a 37-year-old mother of four:

"My life is getting harder each day.... I have a lot of problems, problems with paying gas bill and electricity bill and I am not able to buy things for my children when they want it ... I can't do anything ... I feel very sad and suicidal, want to just terminate my own life, but because of the children I cannot do anything." (Bangladeshi)

Speaking of how they coped with these problems, many participants expressed a sense of resignation about their circumstances. A common strategy among participants was to compare their own situation with somebody else's so that their own problems would not seem so difficult.

It was common for many participants to accept unhappy events as their fate ("These are the facts of life, to move on and carry on"). Acceptance of fate was sometimes explicitly linked to religious beliefs. Many participants reported that they practised their faith on a regular basis, by saying prayers and observing religious rituals. Champa's faith strongly influenced the view that she took of her illness as well as how she dealt with it, after an encounter with what she saw as 'black magic':

"For the last five years I've been like this, in this condition of illness. But I haven't shown my real illness to anyone because of all this magic things ... you are aware, in our culture, in Islam or in India, you understand, there is magic, black magic is there. They have been done on me. The elders we know have the knowledge that my illness, that in doctors' eyes came to me as illness, is black magic. Because of their prayers, their treatment, there is much change in me." (Muslim)

Champa's words also clearly demonstrate her conviction that appropriate treatment for her condition is spiritual and not medical.

## Views on the difference between talking to a counsellor and family/friends

Asked whether they could see any benefit in talking to a counsellor as opposed to a family member or friend, non-clients of counselling were mixed in their response. On the one hand, they were conscious of the limitations of support from family and friends, most noticeably possible lapses in confidentiality. However, on the other hand, they felt that relatives and friends often shared a common background and cultural values which considerably enhanced communication, attributes which they seemed to think would not be found in counsellors.

Other participants felt that there would be value in talking to a neutral and professionally trained person, who would enable them to deal with the issues they were facing ("Certain things you have to do outside. Got to have professional help, in my opinion"). This view was expressed by an overwhelming majority of clients, who considered talking to a trained 'outsider' easier than talking to a member of their family or a close friend. However, there were also a small minority of non-clients who felt that if the purpose of counselling was not to provide advice or guidance, there was little value in using the service.

## Summary
- The majority of the participants had either family members or friends whom they could talk to about their problems. However, in times of crisis these people were not always seen to be the best confidants. Consequently, the informal support that could be gained from them was limited.
- While the overwhelming majority of former counselling clients were positive about the benefits of such professional support, non-clients were mixed in their views of its potential usefulness. Many felt that talking to someone who was of the same cultural background and who shared their cultural values and norms was very important. They seemed to think that this would not be possible within a counselling service.

# Experiences of counselling

A key element of this study has been to review participants' counselling experiences in order to inform the planning and delivery of culturally sensitive counselling services for Asian people. Drawing on the accounts of 19 past clients, this chapter considers the circumstances which led them to seek counselling, how they accessed it, their knowledge, expectations and experience of the service, their views of counsellors and the impact of counselling on their lives.

In this participant group, there were nine men and 10 women, ranging in age from 24 to 61. The majority were married with children, while three were divorced and four single. All spoke English as well as one or more Asian languages, with nine registering English as their first language. Half were students or in paid employment while the rest were either retired, unemployed or looking after their homes and children.

## Circumstances leading to the uptake of counselling

The circumstances which led participants to seek counselling generally involved considerable pain and distress. Some participants recounted how bereavement and multiple bereavement of close relatives had led to depression, relationship breakdown and stress. They spoke of their extreme difficulties in accepting the death of loved ones, their great sense of loss and their own struggle to continue living.

When Asif, who described himself as a Pakistani-Scot, lost his son in a tragic accident, his sense of loss and sorrow resulted initially in difficulties in sleeping. This was then followed by a 'deep depression' which led his wife to contact a GP

who referred him for counselling. Raj, too, experienced depression when his father died and his sister committed suicide soon after. Within six months of these events, his wife also lost two members of her family:

"And as an outcome of bereavement, there were lots of issues which were affected, my studies were affected. Our relationship, my wife and myself, though we are a highly compatible intellectual couple ... we could not come across to each other, and that was affected, and our social life was affected as a result of that." (Indian)

In some cases, the feelings of pain and distress were manifested physically. Karima's case is a typical example. When she lost her mother, she experienced "anxiety and depression as well, mental and physical, both".

Alcohol abuse, in most cases related to some other significant event such as a bereavement or redundancy, often led to depression and stress. In some cases, it also led to uncontrolled behaviour. It was often a cause of marital and familial tension. This was the case with Gopal, who had to deal with the closure of his company and the death of his mother within a short period of time. Unable to talk about his feelings, he sought escape through alcohol, which sometimes led to aggressive behaviour.

Problems at work or job loss also brought about serious psychological and physical ailments for a few respondents, yet the desire to cope and be strong remained powerful. As Rani explains:

"Because actually this problem started
from my work, you know, when I left my
work ... but at the same time I am
thinking, why can't I with myself be
brave, and brave and brave, you know,
fight, instead of depending on tablets ...
sometimes I am really feeling very bad in
the morning, I don't feel like getting up,
and sometimes I think 'what's the point of
living in this world'." (Indian)

A few respondents faced relationship breakdowns,
which led ultimately to divorce and significant
upheaval in their lives. One of their main
concerns at this time was a desire to preserve
some semblance of normality and continue as if
nothing untoward had happened. Often, this was
achieved at a high personal cost. For example,
Shahida (age 44) refrained from telling her family
about the gradual breakdown of her marriage.
When questioned by family members about her
loss of weight, she deflected their concerns by
explaining that she was dieting.

On moving away from the family for the first time
and facing the disintegration of the support
networks she had been accustomed to, Zabi (aged
24) experienced considerable stress and anxiety:

"At home it's like, you know, I have quite
a close-knit family even though I may not
be able to talk to them I know they are
there ... my lifestyle was really stable and
like, when I came away from home, that
kind of, like all fell to pot...." (Pakistani)

It was evident that many of the participants had
had to cope with difficult life events such as
bereavement, relationship or marital breakdown,
redundancy and separation from family. This had
a major impact on their psychological state and
had led them, their families or an involved
professional to recognise that professional support
would be beneficial.

## Access to counselling

Prior to accessing counselling, the majority of
client-participants either knew nothing or very
little about such services. Going for counselling
was thus not an option that they immediately
considered. In most cases, someone within the
family or circle of friends was instrumental in
suggesting it as a means of dealing with the

situation. Generally, the same person was
instrumental in facilitating the process by locating
a service and arranging the first appointment.

Some clients were recommended for counselling
by their GPs. In some of these cases, the GP made
the initial appointment on behalf of the client.
Often, such arrangements were made by the GP
without consulting the client. A few participants
had been referred to counselling by their
employers.

Self-referrals were few and generally came about
because the individuals concerned had some prior
knowledge of counselling. Some self-referrers
reported that they had faced considerable
problems in locating an appropriate agency or
counsellor:

"We talked to our doctor, and the doctor
said that they could arrange for some
counselling.... But when I asked a second
question, 'was it culturally sensitive', the
answer was not comfortable ... he himself
did not know where such services would
be available.... My wife is a social worker,
so she had to use her network, right, to
try and locate it." (Raj, Indian)

Raj's account suggests that there is insufficient
knowledge among professionals (for instance,
GPs and social workers) of the range of
counselling services which are available. This
limits their ability to refer clients to the most
appropriate services.

Other difficulties which hindered participants'
access to counselling were physical distance, cost
and uncertainty about the ability of such services
to meet their needs. A few participants also spoke
of the stigma attached to mental health problems
and their fear of being labelled as someone who
had 'lost it'. This fear was particularly acute in
communities that were small and close-knit.

## Knowledge, understanding and expectations of counselling

Initially, a substantial number of clients had little
or no knowledge of counselling. Consequently,
some had either no expectations of the service at
all or were unclear about the process and what
might be achieved. However, most had a vague
feeling that they would benefit in some way. For

example, Khalid felt that once he went for treatment, "something would be done". Raksha, on the other hand, thought that "somebody would wave a magic wand" and sort her problems out. Others were simply hoping for some ease in the distress, anxiety and pain that they were experiencing.

A few who had heard about counselling from friends, had a better understanding of the service:

> "They will only listen to you, will not advise you ... so one goes there and unburdens one's heart." (Ali, Asian-Scottish)

On the other hand, some participants had very clear expectations of the service. Noori felt a need for someone who would hear what she was saying and "perhaps label these things, put them into boxes and give me a framework that I could work with". Similarly, Mamta wanted the counsellor to help her to come out of her depression, to view her dilemma from a fresh perspective and enable her to arrive at a means of coping with the situation.

Having experienced counselling, participants achieved a personal clarity concerning the purpose and process of counselling. Some saw it as a space for expressing and defining concerns as well as achieving some sort of resolution to their problems ("It's about expressing one's anxieties and bringing out a solution"). Others viewed it as a means of exploring the self in depth, enabling them to develop and cope with problems. Ram, for example, saw counselling as a process "confined within boundaries which enabled a person to develop positively".

## Experiences of counselling

The majority of the respondents had had a positive experience of counselling. They felt that the service provided them with a safe and comforting environment in which it became easy to talk to the counsellor:

> "I used to talk about what was in my heart, tell her all my pain. My heart felt very comfortable because all the lava brimming in my heart, I took it out. One realises that there is someone to listen to my pain." (Ali, Asian-Scottish)

It was clear that the experience of being allowed to express their feelings in the presence of an understanding individual brought participants considerable comfort and relief. Participants' trust in the confidential nature of the service encouraged them to talk freely about their situation.

Some participants talked about their feelings of discomfort with having to face up to certain issues. Nevertheless, they found the sessions helpful and/or cathartic.

> "He was on the ball, so sometimes I felt real discomfort, but I knew the more uncomfortable I felt, the greater the need to go back." (Ram, Indian)

## Views on counselling sessions and counsellors

In the majority of cases, the counselling was conducted in English. Most of the participants were satisfied with this as they were comfortable speaking in English and would have found certain things difficult to explain in an Asian language. However, others found the inability to talk in their own Asian language restricted their ability to fully express themselves and seriously affected the quality of the experience:

> "... after three times counselling, I ask her not to come because with my own language, I feel more peaceful talking in my own language ... because there are few things which you can't explain ... I can't." (Salma, Pakistani)

Those who had worked with an Asian counsellor often switched between the two languages. For example, the session might start off in English but to explain something specific the client would switch to, say, Punjabi, and then revert to English.

The majority of participants expressed satisfaction with their counsellor, seeing them as 'caring', 'professional', and able to listen and fully understand their problems. Shahida recalled that although her Scottish counsellor did not have any knowledge of her customs and traditions, she was "willing to learn". However, Rahim, who had a female Asian counsellor, felt that his counsellor was able to "understand better", since she spoke the same language as him and shared similar customs.

For a few respondents, the issues of power and control were acutely worrying factors. Expecting the client–counsellor relationship to be one in which both were equals, Zabi was dismayed to find that she often felt inferior and intimidated. For other participants, there was some dissatisfaction around the time boundary that was set. This was found to be somewhat inhibiting for a few clients who felt that it limited the depth and quality of the experience. For example, Rani felt that her half-hour sessions were completely inadequate to describe what she was going through.

A few participants felt that their counsellor had failed to assess their situation adequately, giving rise to feelings of frustration and helplessness. At least one participant attributed the failure to understand to prejudice on the part of the counsellor and felt offended by it:

> "This guy made me feel uncomfortable thinking about, as I said, like 'where has she crawled out from'." (Raksha, Scottish-Sikh).

## Impact of counselling

For the majority of participants, counselling proved to be a comforting and beneficial experience. Participants were able to open up to the counsellor, unburden, talk through things they had been unable to express to even their closest friends or family and resolve some long-standing issues. For example, counselling made Ali feel 'lighter in the heart' and able to look to the future.

Some participants reported that counselling had had a long-term constructive impact in enabling them to build up self-esteem and create a greater sense of control over their lives. This was certainly the case for Mamta:

> "Emotionally you feel inside, you are coping well. You feel better. You get control over your emotions ... more confidence. No feeling low ... generally I feel very good." (Asian)

Counselling also enabled some participants to develop their ability to understand themselves and their situation more clearly and to develop strategies for coping more effectively.

For some, counselling was also a liberating experience, allowing them to pour out their problems, and leaving them feeling free and relieved. These participants clearly appreciated the time and space to explore personal issues and the opportunity to fully express how they felt. Nari, for instance, who had been preoccupied and worried about how members of her family were coping with the loss of another family member, was only able to give vent to her own feelings within her counselling sessions.

Interestingly, several participants reported that the experience of counselling had alleviated physical symptoms, such as panic attacks, chest pain, coughing fits and inability to sleep. In some cases, the effect was immediate. In Nari's words:

> "When I left the room and he said to me, 'How are you feeling now?'. And I said, 'Oh, a lot better'. I just come out and then after that, there was no temperature, no chesty cough, nothing ... I slept right through at night-time." (Indian)

While the majority of men found counselling had a positive impact, about half the women found the experience to have been of limited value. For most, the dissatisfaction arose from being mismatched with a counsellor who did not meet their needs or preferences. Concern was expressed not only about the lack of suitability of the counsellor with regard to ethnicity but also about the lack of consultation in the process:

> "They went out of their way to find me an Asian doctor [psychiatrist] which was sort of stupid ... I wouldn't have liked to have an Asian doctor even if he could speak my language. I would have preferred it if they'd told me, 'Well this is who we've found', I would have said 'No', and it would have saved me the trauma...." (Raksha, Scottish-Sikh)

In contrast, some clients who did not have a counsellor from their own ethnic background felt that little had been gained from the experience. A few participants expressed some dissatisfaction with their experience of counselling which they linked explicitly to the gender of the counsellor ("I just didn't feel comfortable talking to a man").

However, even a few of these participants felt that they had benefited in some way through counselling. While Karima found she was less confused, Raksha asserted that, although her experience of counselling was difficult and limited, it had made her stronger.

## Summary

- Clients' knowledge and understanding of counselling services were very low prior to their use of the service. The circumstances which led participants to seek counselling were generally major life events such as death in the family, marital or relationship breakdown, redundancy and separation from the family.
- The GPs and other professionals involved were not fully aware of the range of counselling services which were available to meet the specific needs of different groups. As a result, they were unable to refer clients to appropriate services.
- For the majority of participants, the impact of counselling has been overwhelmingly positive. Counselling provided them with time and space to explore personal issues and feelings in a safe environment, build self-esteem and confidence, and deal with their problems.
- The key factors which would enable clients to maximise the potential benefits of counselling are: consultation on their preferences for a counsellor, allowing them a greater sense of control within the sessions and a genuine engagement on the part of the counsellor in understanding their circumstances and feelings.

# 4

# Expectations and preferences for service delivery

Clients' and non-clients' expectations and preferences for counsellors and counselling sessions are vitally important factors to consider in the planning and delivery of culturally sensitive services. It is important to note that although many clients did not have clear expectations initially, as they became more familiar with the process, they developed clear preferences concerning several aspects of the service. Failure to fully consider these views is likely to result in dissatisfaction and low use of the service. In this chapter, we consider what participants expect from their counsellors and their preferences for important aspects of the service. Finally, we examine the factors which clients and non-clients feel would facilitate access to counselling services.

## Essential qualities of counsellors

Generally, participants were very articulate in their expectations of their counsellors:

> "Their role is ... not just to listen but ... to make the person think of other possibilities and reasons why they are going through this crisis." (Bushra, age 32, Scottish-Asian)

> "[Counsellor] must have something ... which is healing, supportive ... encouraging, which gives hope, which gives off positive vibes, and this is what I mean by healing." (Noori, age 33, Indian)

> "Counsellor has to be patient, polite and know how to approach problems and never ever show them that he is like a teacher, sitting over and above them in asking questions, treat his or her equal,

that's important." (Asif, age 61, Pakistani-Scottish)

Irrespective of age, gender or ethnicity, it was clear that participants wanted their counsellors to be actively engaged, demonstrate a positive attitude towards them and treat them with respect.

## Ethnicity of the counsellor and language of counselling

About half of all participants did not see the ethnicity of the counsellor in itself as an important issue. The remaining participants had either a strong preference for an Asian counsellor or, conversely, a strong aversion to a counsellor from their own ethnic background. Raj, who had lived in the UK for 10 years, spent six months tracking down an agency which provided counselling specifically for Asian people. Explaining his preference for an Asian counsellor, Raj felt that a non-Asian counsellor might, after some time, reach an understanding of his different cultural values, family structures and dynamics. However, he was not confident that they would fully understand how these values and systems were actively translated and experienced.

Those who preferred not to have a counsellor from the same ethnic background spoke about their reluctance to reveal their personal circumstances to someone who might know them or their family personally. For some, a fear of being judged on the basis of the cultural norms and values of their community which they do not share, was another critical factor. Ram, aged 33 and born in the UK, said:

"If I'm going to go out and see someone I'm not going to see someone who's like my aunty, I don't want to see someone like that – I don't want to go. Call it my prejudices, or presumptions or whatever." (Indian)

Not surprisingly, clients' preferences for the ethnicity of their counsellor were closely related to their preference for the language of counselling. Where individuals did not feel comfortable speaking in English, they expressed a strong preference for someone who could speak the Asian language(s) in which they could fully express themselves. The use of interpreters in counselling was universally seen to be inappropriate due to the intensely private nature of what would be communicated and related to concerns over confidentiality.

The majority of client-participants, however, were comfortable speaking in English, with several registering English as their first language. Others reported that they were equally comfortable speaking either in English or in an Asian language. However, a few of these people asserted that, faced with the prospect of an Asian-speaking counsellor, who might possibly be known to them, they would opt for an English-speaking counsellor. Regardless of their individual preference, many clients spoke of the important need for counselling to be available in Asian languages. This indicated that they knew of people who were not able to fully communicate in English and who would benefit from counselling provided it was available in an appropriate language.

## Gender of the counsellor

About two thirds of the participants felt that the gender of the counsellor was an important issue, with women expressing a stronger preference for a counsellor of the same gender than men. This preference was linked to a sense of ease and safety ("Our ladies, they are frightened, they are very comfortable with females"). Other women felt that female counsellors would be better able to understand their problems. For some men and women, preference for a counsellor of the same gender was explicitly linked to their religious beliefs.

In spite of a preference for a counsellor of the same gender, the majority of men were less rigid in their gender-related preferences. However, there were some exceptions to this, with some male participants stating that they would prefer a female counsellor. A small minority of female participants also preferred a counsellor of the opposite gender, underlining the need for trained counsellors of both sexes and highlighting the importance of consulting clients on their preferences.

## Age and religion of the counsellor

The overwhelming majority of participants felt that the age of the counsellor was very important, relating it to greater maturity and experience in dealing with problems. Mamta (age 45) who had seen an Asian counsellor of about her own age, expressed a typical view:

"I would rather have an experienced person rather than a very young 20-year-old. Because age and experience also makes a person very rich and all the training and understanding helps them to relate to their own age and experience as well." (Asian)

Interestingly, the counsellor's religion was unanimously viewed as totally unimportant. This was particularly striking, given the great importance that religion played in the lives of some of the participants.

## Preferences for venue

Most of the clients had received counselling in a voluntary sector agency while a few had seen a counsellor at a GP's surgery, hospital, university or at work. They were largely satisfied with the location, with only a few complaining of having to travel a long distance.

In contrast, non-clients varied significantly in their preferred location. Just under half of the non-clients identified the home as their preferred venue. In addition to feeling that it provided a comfortable and safe environment, other reasons given for this preference included the difficulty of leaving the house. As Simeela, who cares for a disabled child, makes clear:

"A younger woman has children to look after in the house or has to bring the children from nursery, or go to school, so they won't have time on their hands to go. It's easier for them to talk in their own house, while the older woman has time. They can go to different centres or hospitals … unless they are very depressed and they are not coming out of the house, then the counsellor has to go to them." (Pakistani-Asian-Muslim)

On the other hand, a few non-client participants stated they would prefer counselling sessions to be held outside their homes. This was either linked to the desire for a change of environment or privacy from other family members.

Both clients and non-clients were comfortable with agencies catering for both men and women, with only a minority of female clients identifying a women-only agency as their preference. Some participants felt that counselling should either be located within GP surgeries or should be community-based to ensure easy and affordable access to the service.

## Length and frequency of sessions

Almost none of the past clients had been able to decide the length of their sessions, and only a few had been able to agree it jointly with their counsellor. Sessions were usually of 50 to 60 minutes fixed duration. Only one participant reported that the length of her sessions was flexible, and varied according to her needs. Overall, however, the overwhelming majority of past clients were satisfied with the length of their sessions.

Participants had a greater influence when it came to deciding the frequency of their sessions, with half reporting that they had either decided this themselves or in collaboration with their counsellors. The majority of participants were satisfied with the length of time between sessions, however this was arrived at. A few reported that they were able to contact their counsellor by telephone in between sessions, if they needed to, but that the need had not arisen.

## Increasing access to counselling

Participants generally commented on the low levels of awareness in their communities of counselling. Mamta, a past client who works as a social worker, spoke of the stigma which is related to mental health and counselling and of the importance of counteracting this attitude:

"I feel that people don't recognise or understand what counselling is. So it needs more awareness and publicity … there's stigma about going to a counsellor. People really look at you and feel, 'Why she has to go to a counsellor? He or she was mad'." (Asian)

Some of the suggestions for enhancing awareness of counselling and facilitating access included the implementation of 'telephone-hotlines' and the distribution of leaflets and posters in English and Asian community languages. Importantly, several participants felt that counsellors should do more outreach work to publicise the service and change people's attitude towards mental health problems and the role of counselling services. Suki suggests appropriate locations for 'outreach work':

"Go out like, maybe like temples … or women's groups … and explain to them in Punjabi … and they would understand. I think a lot more people would start using it … you'd have to make them more aware, make the community outside more aware that this service is there, and that there is no way that anybody else would find out, if anybody has used it or not, you know, that kind of confidence building has to be installed in them." (Scottish-Sikh)

## Summary

- Clients value counsellors who treat them with respect, show a genuine interest in them, and who have a real understanding of their problems.

- As familiarity increases, clients develop clear preferences in relation to the ethnicity, gender and age of their counsellors and the language of counselling. Failure to take account of these preferences leads to dissatisfaction and low use.

- The diverse preferences of clients for the ethnicity and gender of the counsellor highlights the importance of providing clients with adequate choice and of consulting clients on their preferences. It also highlights the importance of training all counsellors in racial and cultural awareness.

- Some non-clients expressed a strong preference for counselling to be provided within the home, highlighting the need for increased flexibility in service provision.

- Both clients and non-clients were concerned about the low awareness of the service in their communities. They felt that increased attention should be paid to publicising the existence and nature of counselling services through a variety of means, particularly outreach work.

# 5

# Review of counselling services in the voluntary sector

While counselling provision has expanded rapidly in recent years, the largest growth of service provision has occurred in the voluntary sector. The voluntary sector has traditionally been credited with the ability to respond flexibly and innovatively in meeting users' needs, often providing services which are not offered by statutory organisations. However, it is well known that agencies operating in the sector are limited in their ability to strategically plan their services due to the short-term and limited nature of funding.

In this chapter, we consider the nature of counselling services and the organisational contexts within which they are offered. We also examine their accessibility and sensitivity to the perceptions, needs, experiences and preferences of Asian people as described in Chapters 2, 3 and 4.

## Range of services

The range of services provided by agencies under the banner of 'counselling' varies greatly. The BAC distinguishes between activities recognised as counselling and those identified as utilising 'counselling skills' or 'a counselling approach'. Counselling is understood to take place only when the counsellor and client explicitly agree to enter into a counselling relationship. Counselling skills, on the other hand, may be used to enhance another professional helping role such as social work or vocational guidance or telephone help-line support.

In general, the training requirements and professional obligations of counsellors are more rigorous than for counselling skills practitioners. The former are obliged to adhere to a professional code of ethics, monitor their own practice and have regular ongoing counselling supervision while the latter are not.

Several agencies combine the use of a counselling skills approach with other services, for example, information and advice-giving. Typically, such agencies may sometimes refer to this type of work as 'counselling'. While acknowledging that such services have a useful role to play in certain contexts, we have, for the purposes of our review, chosen to focus on agencies that offer services which are closely aligned with the BAC definition.

## Participating agencies

Ten agencies were identified in Glasgow, Bristol, Leeds and London. These included five agencies which seek to cater for the needs of the whole population and five agencies specifically catering for the needs of one or more minority ethnic groups. For convenience, we shall refer to the former as mainstream organisations and the latter as black-led agencies. In addition, three umbrella organisations with responsibility for planning counselling services and/or providing training in counselling were also examined (see Appendix C for a list of agencies involved in the study).

## What are the sources of client referral?

There are three main sources of referral: external, internal and self-referral. External referrals are usually generated from the agencies' local networks. Several agencies reported that a large number of their referrals come from GPs. Other referral sources vary according to the nature of the service. For example, one agency which provides counselling and advice to young people reported that schools, youth workers and social workers generate a number of their referrals. Another agency, which supports black people with mental health problems, obtains a significant number of their referrals from community mental health teams, consultants at hospitals and from other voluntary organisations.

Internal referrals are common where agencies provide a range of differing services for a particular client group. In these agencies staff may suggest that users of other services go for counselling, if they feel it would be beneficial.

Self-referral is seen as an important means of access. It is closely linked to recommendations by past clients or a person's family and friends.

## How do mainstream agencies explain the low use of counselling by black people?

While all the agencies in our sample expressed a desire to increase uptake of their services by black people, they reported variable rates of success in achieving this. It is interesting to note that where agencies offered more than one type of counselling service, significant variations were reported in the rates of uptake by black people. For example, in one mainstream agency, an informal drop-in service for young people attracted the most culturally diverse group of clients.

Mainstream agencies reported that several factors impacted on their ability to successfully attract black clients, notably:

- the ethnic composition of the local population;
- the ethnic composition of the counselling team;
- the limited and short-term nature of funding;
- structural factors such as institutional racism.

Nevertheless, given that the agencies were located in areas with a relatively dense population of minority ethnic people, the low use of most agencies' services by black people, including Asian people, was disturbing.

## What efforts do agencies make to publicise their services?

While black-led agencies tend to carry out considerable outreach work, there was little evidence that the majority of mainstream agencies invested time or effort to publicise their services to black communities. Indeed, a few of these agencies expressed some concern about actively publicising their services to the latter because of their long waiting lists or, in one case, uncertainty about their ability to meet the needs of these clients.

## What issues lead clients to seek counselling?

All agencies reported that it was common to find clients initially presenting with one problem while other equally important, or more important, issues would only be revealed later. Among the generic counselling services the most common issues identified were:

- depression;
- marital and relationship difficulties;
- domestic violence;
- alcohol abuse;
- self-harm;
- sexual abuse.

Agencies specialising in drug or alcohol work found that a dependency problem was often symptomatic of other underlying issues, including unemployment, bereavement and relationship difficulties. Furthermore, alcohol and/or drug dependency could lead to other problems, such as marital breakdown and criminality.

In addition, the issues reported by those agencies serving a large number of Asian clients included issues such as living with an extended family, resistance to and difficulties resulting from arranged marriage, and inter-generational conflict.

## How sensitively do agencies work with difference?

In the UK, counsellors are generally trained in one or more of a number of theoretical orientations. Of these, the most common are the person-centred and psychodynamic counselling approaches. Most black and mainstream agencies were confident that, regardless of their theoretical orientation, they would be able to offer a sensitive service to black people since their counsellors were trained to respect and work with the diverse views of their individual clients, including their cultural and religious beliefs:

> "... it's really being very pro-active and mindful of the client's wishes and needs, whichever model or theoretical base we use." (Director, black counselling agency)

However, it was significant that agencies varied in the extent to which they felt that an intimate knowledge of the cultural background, values and religious systems of their black clients was important. Although a few mainstream agencies lacked confidence in their ability to work with black clients and were concerned about their lack of experience in the area, the generally held view was that what the counsellor needed to know would emerge in their work with individual clients. This tendency of mainstream agencies to trust that issues about race, culture or religion would surface within the context of counselling sessions and that individual counsellors would then 'learn' the relevance of these issues for their clients was worrying. There appeared to be little awareness of the impact of racism or other social factors that are likely to contribute to psychological distress.

In contrast, counsellors working in black agencies were quick to point out that, although their views and values often differed substantially from those of their clients, they felt that they were able to offer a service that was finely tuned to their clients' needs. They attributed this to their extensive experience of working with clients from one or more minority ethnic backgrounds, which had led them to develop certain distinct practices.

## Flexible approach in meeting clients' needs

Black-led agencies tend to adopt a more flexible approach in enabling their clients to deal with their difficulties. For example, many reported that, in their experience, Asian clients often expected to be given advice. While some agencies strongly resisted all attempts to elicit advice, others were prepared to offer some in the initial stages with a view to progressing towards greater autonomy as

the relationship developed. Depending on the needs of the client and the organisational context, some counsellors would also be willing to act as advocates to facilitate access to other services.

In addition, many black-led agencies actively sought to work with their clients' families where they felt that the issues their clients faced were closely bound up with those of their family members. Counsellors often took on the role of family mediator or conciliator, providing a safe space for family members to listen and communicate with each other and work together towards a deeper understanding and respect for each other's views. Although mainstream agencies expressed a willingness to work with members of the family if this was desired by the client, it was clear that this was not common practice.

## What arrangements are made for counselling sessions?

There were few significant differences between black and mainstream agencies in the contractual arrangements for counselling. Table 1 summarises the main details.

## How do agencies cater for language requirements?

Where clients do not feel comfortable speaking in English, the ability of the counsellor to speak the client's first language is crucial. Most black-led agencies were able to offer counselling in a number of community languages as well as English and, as a result, were widely successful in meeting this need.

Most mainstream agencies either did not have any counsellors who were able to speak Asian languages or an extremely small number of such counsellors. Furthermore, several took the view that Asian clients who wished to work with a counsellor who spoke their mother tongue would either contact an Asian agency themselves or would be referred there. A recurring theme expressed by mainstream agencies in support of their largely 'English language only' provision was that black clients often expressed a preference to see someone who was *not* from their own community or from a similar cultural background. This was linked to concerns about loss of confidentiality. While this view was supported by some of the client participants in the study, many others confirmed that they would be more comfortable speaking in an Asian language.

Service provision by mainstream agencies which is based on the assumption that black people who cannot speak English, or prefer not to, will be served by black agencies appears to be an abdication of responsibility. Furthermore, such a view is of particular concern given the low number of black agencies providing counselling in the UK and the complete absence of such services in many parts of the country.

## How able are counselling agencies to meet specific preferences?

In both mainstream and black agencies, there were considerable limitations with respect to the degree of choice available to clients. As had emerged in the interviews with participants, the agencies reported that female clients generally exhibit a stronger preference for seeing a counsellor of their own gender than their male counterparts. Nevertheless, since most counsellors are female, some agencies experienced difficulty in accommodating men who wished to see a male counsellor. Interestingly, in at least one of the Asian agencies reviewed, the preference of female counsellors to work with female clients is also taken into account.

**Table 1: Summary of contractual arrangements**

| | |
|---|---|
| Location of services | Counselling is normally delivered on the agency premises, although some agencies are prepared to see clients in their own homes either initially or, in exceptional circumstances, thereafter. In many Asian agencies, 'telephone counselling' is also available to those who find it difficult to leave their homes. These agencies reported that due to the limited availability of appropriate support in the UK, they also receive calls from other parts of the country. |
| Initial meeting | Agencies commonly offer an introductory or assessment session at which the needs of the client are explored and the nature of the service is explained. Agencies vary in the length of time clients may have to wait between this initial meeting and their first counselling session. |
| Counsellor allocation | Agencies usually allocate clients to counsellors on the basis of availability. The nature and severity of the problem are key factors in identifying a counsellor with an appropriate level of skill and experience. Where specific client preferences are expressed at the initial session, these are accommodated when possible (see the section on meeting specific preferences, pp 21-2). |
| Length and timing of counselling sessions | Counselling is usually conducted in weekly sessions of 50 or 60 minutes. Although some agencies are prepared to maintain client contact between sessions in cases of particular difficulty, this is not usually encouraged. |
| Duration of counselling | Agencies vary in whether or not they normally restrict clients to a maximum number of counselling sessions. Nevertheless, all agencies acknowledged that some clients require long-term work, for example, those who have experienced sexual abuse or other severe childhood traumas. However, contracts which exceed a year are extremely rare. |

Consequently, clients who express a particular preference for a counsellor may face a conflict between the urgency of their situation and the amount of time it may take to meet their expectations. As a result, clients are often faced with either accepting what is available or being put on a waiting list:

> "So if they want to see a woman or they want to see a man or they want to see a Bangladeshi counsellor or whatever, we will try and meet that wherever it is possible. Sometimes that means we end up saying to them, 'You have a choice, yes, we have a male Afro-Caribbean counsellor that you can see, but if you want to see him you have to wait six weeks. If you want to see someone sooner than this, this is what we can offer'." (Coordinator, mainstream agency)

## How are services evaluated?

Most counsellors build in an initial review session between the third and sixth sessions to monitor the effectiveness of the counselling process for the client. They usually also conduct a final review and incorporate periodic reviews in ongoing, longer-term work.

However, few of the agencies had put into place any formal mechanisms for obtaining client feedback either when counselling was completed or at some interval following the final session. Nor did they seek to obtain feedback from clients who did not attend their initial meeting or who failed to return for later sessions. In general, the effectiveness of service provision was rather simplistically judged, largely in terms of the number of referrals and clients' willingness to complete their therapeutic courses.

Furthermore, although the counselling agencies generally maintain basic records of their clients, they do not conduct ethnic monitoring of their service. As a result, they have no access to the following valuable information pertaining to their black clients:

- the nature of problems which lead such clients to seek counselling;
- the routes by which they access the service;
- the numbers of counselling sessions used;
- the proportion of clients who complete

therapeutic sessions to the satisfaction of both the client and the counsellor;
- specific interventions which facilitate the process and those which hinder it.

Designing effective evaluation mechanisms raises some challenging ethical issues concerning the precise nature of the process, maintenance of confidentiality and respect for client autonomy. Nevertheless, the need to address these difficulties must be seen in the context of the importance of improving service provision and quality for all sections of the population.

## How do agencies train and select counsellors?

The training requirement for a professional counsellor is typically at diploma level. The relationship between training providers and agencies varies. Some of the larger agencies provide their own training programmes which their counsellors undertake. Most locally-based agencies, however, do not have access to in-house training and recruit trained counsellors and/ or trainees from a variety of programmes.

Mainstream agencies consider the 'cultural mix' of their counselling staff to be of considerable importance in their ability to attract clients from diverse cultural backgrounds. As a result, a key issue for several mainstream agencies is their capacity to recruit counsellors from diverse backgrounds:

> "One of the things that was clear to us from the very beginning was that if we were going to provide a service to the Bangladeshi community, then we needed to have Bangladeshi counsellors." (Coordinator, mainstream agency)

The agency cited above acted on this recognition by recruiting a new member of staff with relevant skills and experience and then providing them with training in counselling. However, this practice appeared to be the exception rather than the norm, with other agencies relying on encouraging black people to undertake training.

## How adequately are counsellors prepared and supported?

All accredited counselling training programmes provide some input on cultural difference, although the extent and breadth of such input varies considerably. In addition, both black and mainstream agencies seek to address issues of cultural difference within the wider context of continuing professional development. This is generally conducted within the context of ongoing supervision and periodic in-service training.

Counsellors in several black-led agencies expressed concern over the suitability of currently available counsellor training for adequately preparing people to work with clients from diverse communities:

> "We learn about all these theories which don't actually apply to 90% of our clients.... In practice, what do you do faced with a client who is completely different from what you ever learnt about?" (Coordinator, black counselling agency)

Generally, agencies reported that the professional requirements for supervision were being met and were working well; that supervisors were often experienced practitioners who had undertaken training in supervision; and that their experience helped to ensure adequate awareness of racial and cultural difference.

## Summary

- While all agencies expressed a willingness to increase use of their services by black clients, there was little evidence on the part of most mainstream agencies of any strategy to specifically target black communities in their efforts to publicise their services.
- Some mainstream agencies reported that they were wary of publicising their services more widely, because of their inability to meet the demands of existing clients or their lack of confidence in meeting the needs of black clients.
- While all black-led agencies felt that it was important to have a deep understanding of the racial and cultural background of their clients, many mainstream agencies felt that issues about race, culture or religion would emerge in counselling sessions and that counsellors would learn the significance of these issues from their clients.
- In general, agencies' ability to provide clients with choice with respect to counsellors, language and location for counselling was limited.
- The tendency of mainstream agencies to trust that black agencies would cater to the needs of those who did not speak English was disturbing, given the very limited availability of black counselling agencies.
- Agencies commonly did not carry out ethnic monitoring, obtain formal feedback from clients who had failed to attend sessions or follow up clients who had completed counselling. Valuable information about the nature of problems faced by black clients, their routes of referral and their satisfaction with the service was thus not available.
- Although mainstream agencies expressed willingness to recruit black counsellors, generally, little effort had been put into how they might actively encourage black applicants.
- Several black counsellors expressed concern about the adequacy of existing training courses in preparing counsellors for meeting the needs of black clients.

# 6

# Conclusions and policy implications

In the light of the growing recognition of the value of counselling and the rapid expansion of counselling services in the last two decades, the continuing low uptake of counselling services by black people is a matter for concern. In this chapter, we draw on the findings which have emerged from the earlier chapters and set out suggestions for improving policy and practice. While the specific focus of this study has been on Asian people, the implications which follow are broadly relevant to increasing the uptake and use of counselling services among other black people.

## Barriers which inhibit access to appropriate counselling

Our findings suggest that low awareness of the existence and the nature of such services among Asian people is a major barrier. Once Asian people are aware of counselling services, negative preconceptions of counselling may hinder their uptake of the service, for example:

- counselling is only intended for the white population;
- counselling is only provided by white people;
- counsellors who come from a different cultural background would not be able to understand their problems.

Self-referrals among Asian people tend to be low. Our findings suggest that Asian people tend to access counselling only at crisis points, when their distress reaches such proportions as to merit concern among friends, family members, employers or GPs, who may then suggest counselling.

Importantly, the low use of counselling services by Asian people also indicates that there is a low referral rate from GPs and other potential referrers. This supports the view that GPs and other referrers either frequently fail to diagnose mental health problems in this client group, are unaware of the relevance of counselling for them or do not know of appropriate services. In this context, the failure of mainstream counselling providers to carry out outreach work in black communities and with potential referrers is particularly worrying.

Our findings strongly suggest that Asian clients, like many other clients, prefer access to services which are not biased by stereotypical views of what is appropriate. However, while there are some areas where Asian clients' needs and preferences are being met by agencies, there are several areas where there are either gaps or mismatches (see the Summary of findings on page vi). Consequently, it is difficult to avoid the conclusion that while, in general, most agencies are guided by the principles of affording maximum choice, flexibility and control to their clients, in practice they are limited in what they can offer. This is particularly the case for black clients, even in geographical areas where there is a relatively high, visible black presence.

## Recommendations for improving practice and policy

The suggestions set out below are directed towards funders, policy makers, potential referrers, training providers, community-based organisations and agencies which provide counselling. Our findings suggest that mainstream agencies have to work much harder than black-led agencies to address the low use of counselling services by black people. All those involved in the planning and delivery of mental health services from the earliest stages of diagnosis to 'after-care' following discharge from institutional care have a variety of approaches at their disposal to improve service provision for black people. These approaches need to be rooted in an equal opportunities policy, which acknowledges the potential for discrimination not only on the basis of 'race', but also gender, disability and sexual orientation.

## Being clear about 'counselling'

A wide range of services exist which are referred to as 'counselling', from the giving of practical information and advice to the therapeutic work which is the focus of this study. To ensure that clients receive the most appropriate service for their needs, it is crucial that:

- Policy makers, funding bodies and potential referrers are aware of the precise nature of the range of available services which are described as counselling, and their various strengths and limitations (distinguishing between 'counselling' and the use of 'counselling skills').
- Agencies are transparent about the nature of the service they offer to their clients and make appropriate referrals, where necessary.

## Increasing *access* to counselling services

Below we describe three key steps which will facilitate increased access to counselling by black people:

- increase the numbers of external referrals;
- encourage a greater number of self-referrals;
- make counselling services more directly accessible.

### Increase the numbers of external referrals of black people

A strategy to increase the referral rate would most appropriately be initiated by counselling providers in collaboration with potential referrers. It would seek to involve GPs, community psychiatric nurses (CPNs), health visitors, social workers and others whose professional and personal contacts are likely to bring them into contact with black people.

---

**Key questions for referrers**

- Are we familiar with the range and nature of counselling services in our catchment area?

- Do we know which services are most adequately prepared to meet the specific needs of black people?

- Do we ethnically monitor our referral rates to ensure that the needs of black people are not being missed or overlooked?

**Key questions for providers**

- Do we liaise with other agencies that may be in contact with potential clients, such as psychiatric services or agencies which provide information and/or advice?

- Do we liaise with black-led voluntary organisations and projects in statutory organisations which specialise in work with black communities?

- Should we specifically identify, and liaise with, professionals who are themselves from a minority ethnic background?

---

*Encourage a greater number of self-referrals*

A carefully designed communications or outreach strategy by providers would go a long way towards raising the awareness of black communities of counselling services and would contribute to an increase in self-referrals.

### Elements of a communication/outreach strategy

- Which minority ethnic group should we target first?

- Have we conducted outreach work in appropriate areas and publicised our services through a variety of channels, such as notices in GP surgeries, schools, shops?

- Have we liaised with relevant black community-based organisations, religious leaders and other community leaders?

- Have we clearly explained the nature and purpose of counselling?

- Have we made clients aware of the benefits they can expect from the service?

- Have we emphasised the confidential nature of the service?

- Does the 'public face' of our organisation, for example, literature about available services, publications in waiting rooms, composition of staff, reflect its intention to make its services accessible to all sections of the population?

*Make counselling services more directly accessible to black communities*

Provision of more flexible services by mainstream providers is likely to increase the uptake of counselling by black people.

### Questions for mainstream counselling providers to consider

- Could we work with black-led voluntary organisations in organising information days, introductory sessions or regular surgeries within their agencies?

- Would we be willing to meet with the client at home, at least initially?

- Do we have the resources to provide a 'drop-in' facility or a telephone hotline?

## Increasing the *appropriateness* of counselling services for black communities

The White Paper *Caring for people* (DoH, 1989) explicitly recognised the merits of planning community-based services in consultation with people from minority ethnic communities. Our findings confirm that participants value being consulted with respect to various elements of the counselling process. Our research also suggests that four key steps can be taken to increase the appropriateness of counselling services:

- increase the number of trained counsellors from diverse communities;
- increase the availability of culturally sensitive provision;
- increase inter-agency collaboration;
- review service provision.

*Increase the number of counsellors from black communities*

This study revealed that some of the least satisfactory counselling experiences occurred when clients' preferences with regard to the ethnicity and gender of the counsellor and the language of counselling were not met. It is important that agencies are not only able to provide clients with appropriate choice but that their composition reflects the diverse communities which they serve.

### Key questions for counselling providers

- Do we have enough trained counsellors from black communities? If not, how can we increase the numbers of these counsellors?

- Do our selection criteria make it difficult for such applicants to be recruited?

- Can we provide counselling training to suitable applicants with relevant skills who do not possess the necessary academic qualifications?

- Can we actively encourage increased applications from black people, for example by providing bursaries or other forms of financial support?

- Are there sources of funding that we can access in order to increase the numbers of trained black counsellors?

## Increase the availability of culturally sensitive provision

Our research revealed that most mainstream agencies tend to trust that issues of race, culture or religion will emerge in the course of the counselling process and that the relevance of these issues for their clients can then be learned. However, it is perhaps obvious that counsellors who have been equipped with adequate training in racial and cultural issues are better prepared to work with black clients.

### Important areas for service and training providers to review

- To what extent do counsellors publicise their clients' right to express their preference or dissatisfaction with any aspect of the service?

- To what extent do we recognise that 'cultural sensitivity' is a quality which can be distinguished from the more general sensitivity of counsellors to individual circumstances and feelings?

- Have issues of race and culture been sufficiently integrated into all basic and advanced-level training, alongside issues about gender, disability and sexuality?

- Do we have sufficient input from experienced black counsellors, or other relevantly skilled black professionals, in our training courses?

- Do we provide our trainees with adequate exposure to clients from diverse communities?

- Does our supervision training adequately prepare practitioners for supervising counsellors who work with black clients?

- How can we maximise opportunities for enhancing cultural sensitivity within the context of continuing professional development?

## Improve inter-agency collaboration

Our review of agencies found that individual agencies tend to develop specific areas of expertise as a result of extensive experience of serving particular client groups or dealing with particular issues. Consequently, there is considerable scope for collaborative work between mainstream and black-led agencies.

### Measures to increase collaboration between agencies

- Have we investigated the possibility of organising secondments for staff or placements for volunteers in other agencies?

- Would it be feasible to exchange our experience and expertise with that gained by other relevant organisations through joint training sessions?

## Reviewing service provision

Our study revealed that ethnic monitoring was not routinely carried out by the majority of agencies. This is worrying, particularly in the case of mainstream providers, since agencies can only tell if they are making progress in making their services available to all sections of the population by ethnic monitoring and by actively seeking black people's views and experiences of their services.

### Main areas that providers need to review

Do we ethnically monitor:

- the number of clients?

- the numbers and sources of referrals from other agencies?

- the presenting issues and outcomes (including whether each client does or does not complete therapy)?

- the number of sessions?

- the client's and counsellor's levels of satisfaction with the counselling?

and:

- Do we follow up people who do not complete their course of counselling?

- Do we maintain contact with our clients after their last session to ascertain the long-term impact of the service?

- Have we considered organising focus group discussions with willing clients to obtain feedback about the quality of our service?

## The role of black communities in promoting awareness and acceptability of counselling services

While it is clear that policy makers, referrers and counselling providers can do much to improve services, black communities themselves have an important role to play in encouraging people to seek appropriate support from counselling and other mental health services.

**Three questions for leaders and members of black communities**

- What can be done within our community to examine attitudes to mental health and confront prejudice in this area?

- Do we recognise that seeking professional help in dealing with psychological difficulties is a *positive* strategy?

- How do we support those who seek counselling and other mental health services?

## The role of funders in increasing investment into counselling provision

Efforts to improve counselling services to black communities must be contextualised within the current climate of increasing demand for such services and growing recognition of their value, particularly among medical and other professionals. However, the increases in demand have not been matched by appropriate increases in funding. Our study supports previous research which has shown that voluntary agencies are limited by financial constraints which make it difficult for them to plan and develop their services strategically.

**Key questions for funders**

- Do we recognise the potential for increased investment in counselling to prevent the deterioration of mental health in individuals and the consequential financial impact on health services and society at large?

- Do we enable voluntary counselling agencies to strategically plan and develop their services?

- Do we give agencies enough support to enable them to provide the broad range of services which are required?

# References

Ananthanarayanan, T. (1994) 'Epidemiology of mental illness among Asians in the UK', *British Journal of Hospital Medicine*, vol 52, pp 500-6.

Bhatnagar, K. and Frank, J. (1997) 'Psychatric disorder in elderly people from the Indian sub-continent living in Bradford', *International Journal of Geriatric Psychiatry*, vol 12, pp 907-12.

Birmingham City Council (1995) *An exploration into counselling services for black and ethnic minority women with mental health problems*, Birmingham: School of Social Work, University of Central England.

Bowes, A. and Domokos, M. (1997) 'Pakistani women, general practitioners and health visitors: communication and service access', in A. Bowes and D. Sim (eds) *Perspectives on welfare – the experience of minority ethnic groups in Scotland*, Aldershot: Ashgate, pp 151-69.

Burnett, R., Mallett, R., Bhugra, D., Hutchinson, G. and Leff, J. (1999) 'The first contact of patients with schizophrenia with psychiatric services: social factors and pathways to care in a multi-ethnic population', *Psychological Medicine*, vol 29, pp 475-83.

Busfield, J. (1999) 'Mental health policy: making gender and ethnicity visible', *Policy & Politics*, Special issue: Mental health and social order, vol 27, no 1, pp 57-73.

Copperman, J. and McNamara, J. (1999) 'Institutional abuse in mental health settings', in J. Stanley, J. Manthorpe and B. Penhole (eds) *Institutional abuse*, London: Routledge, pp 152-72.

Cuijpers, P. (1999) 'The effects of family interventions on relatives' burden: a meta-analysis', *Journal of Mental Health*, vol 8, pp 275-85.

D'Ardenne, P. and Mahatani, A. (1989) 'Introducing transcultural counselling', in P. D'Ardenne and A. Mahatani (eds) *Transcultural counselling in action*, London: Sage Publications, pp 1-13.

DoH (Department of Health) (1989) *Caring for people: Community care in the next decade and beyond*, London: HMSO.

DoH (1997) *The framework for mental health services in Scotland*, Edinburgh: The Stationery Office.

DoH (1998) *Our healthier nation*, London: The Stationery Office.

Donaghy, E. (1997) 'Understanding depression in young South Asian women in Scotland', in A. Bowes and D. Sim (eds) *Perspectives on welfare – the experience of minority ethnic groups in Scotland*, Aldershot: Ashgate, pp 187-202.

Fenton, S. and Sadiq-Sangster, A. (1996) 'Culture, relativism and the expression of mental distress: South Asian women in Britain', *Sociology of Health and Illness*, vol 18, pp 66-85.

Hatfield, B., Mohamed, H., Rahim, Z. and Tanweer, H. (1996) 'Mental health and the Asian communities: a local survey', *British Journal of Social Work*, vol 26, pp 315-36.

Jacob, K., Bhugra, D., Lloyd, K. and Mann, A. (1998) 'Common mental disorders, explanatory models and consultation behaviour among Indian women living in the UK', *Journal of the Royal Society of Medicine*, vol 91, pp 66-71.

Kleinmann, A. (1977) 'Depression, somatisation and the new cross-cultural psychiatry', *Social Science and Medicine*, vol 11, pp 3-10.

Littlewood, R. and Lipsedge, M. (1997) *Aliens and alienists*, London: Routledge.

Macran, S., Ross, H., Hardy, G. and Shapiro, D. (1999) 'The importance of considering clients' perspectives in psychotherapy research', *Journal of Mental Health*, vol 8, no 4, pp 325-37.

McKeigue, P. and Karmi, G. (1993) 'Alcohol consumption and alcohol-related problems in Afro-Caribbeans and South Asians in the United Kingdom', *Alcohol and Alcoholism*, vol 28, pp 1-10.

Moodley, R. (1999) 'Psychotherapy with ethnic minorities: a critical review', *Changes*, vol 17, no 2, pp 109-25.

Moodley, R. (2000a) 'Counselling and psychotherapy in a multicultural context: some training issues, part 1', *Counselling*, vol 11, pp 154-7.

Moodley, R. (2000b) 'Counselling and psychotherapy in a multicultural context: some training issues, part 2', *Counselling*, vol 11, pp 221-4.

Netto, G. (1998) '"I forget myself" – the case for the provision of culturally sensitive respite services for minority ethnic communities', *Journal of Public Health Medicine,* vol 20, pp 221-6.

Odell, S., Surtees, P., Wainwright, N., Commander, M. and Sashidharan, S. (1997) 'Determinants of general practitioner recognition of psychological problems in a multi-ethnic inner-city health district', *British Journal of Psychiatry*, vol 171, pp 537-41.

Prosser, D. (1996) 'Suicides by burning in England and Wales', *British Journal of Psychiatry*, vol 168, pp 175-82.

Radia, K. (1996) *Housing and mental health care needs of Asian people*, York: Joseph Rowntree Foundation.

Save the Children (1997) *Mental health, racism and counselling – community views on needs and services*, Newcastle: Save the Children.

Scottish Executive (1999) *Towards a healthier Scotland*, Edinburgh: The Stationery Office.

Sheth, H., Dziewulski, P. and Settle, J. (1994) 'Self-inflicted burns: a common form of suicide in the Asian population. A 10-year retrospective study', *Burns*, vol 20, pp 334-5.

Silveira, E. and Shah, E. (1998) 'Social determinants of psychiatric morbidity and well-being in immigrant elders and whites in East London', *International Journal of Geriatric Psychiatry*, vol 13, pp 801-12.

Tyrrell, H. (1998) *Needs, services and priorities for mental health in Pollokshields, Glasgow: A local perspective*, Glasgow: Save the Children.

Walker, L. (1996) *The counselling needs for Calderdale's ethnic minority groups*, Calderdale: Relate.

Watters, C. (1996) 'Representations and realities: black people, community care and mental illness', in W. Ahmad and K. Atkin (eds) *'Race' and community care*, Buckingham: Open University Press, pp 105-23.

Williams, J. and Keating, F. (1999) 'The abuse of adults in mental health settings', in J. Stanley, J. Manthorpe and B. Penhole (eds) *Institutional abuse*, London: Routledge, pp 130-51.

# Appendix A: Methodology

## Collecting information from participants, and ethical concerns

We carried out interviews with 38 Asian men and women. Here we describe how we identified the people who took part in this study and we discuss some of the ethical issues involved.

Initially, we contacted voluntary organisations providing mental health services and black community centres. Through carrying out personal visits ('putting a face' to the project) and distributing leaflets in English and Asian languages, we established a snowball system through which interviewees were identified. We were also in close contact with Asian community workers who promoted our project among the Asian communities. This 'word-of-mouth' process facilitated the largest number of participants. Additionally, we approached counselling services to assist us in making contact with past clients.

Due to the personal and sensitive nature of the research, all interviews were conducted by two members of the research team. Each interview was carried out at a venue which was decided by the participant. In most cases, this was their home although some participants chose to be interviewed in a quiet space outside their home, for reasons of confidentiality. A few participants were living with people who did not know they had gone for counselling. Participants were asked which language they would prefer the interview to be conducted in and, where necessary, interviews were facilitated by interpreters to ensure effective communication.

All interviewees were informed that they could terminate the interview at any point, and that they could choose not to answer any of the questions.

Interviewees were also assured of complete confidentiality. Recognising that the task of conducting interviews of such a sensitive nature might be emotionally exacting, arrangements were also put into place for the interviewers to be supported through supervision by a counsellor, should this be required.

## Rationale for selection of voluntary sector agencies in the study

Ten agencies were selected for review from Bristol, Leeds, Glasgow and the London boroughs of Tower Hamlets, Hounslow, and Kensington and Chelsea, local authority areas with an Asian population ranging from 1.61% of the total population in Bristol to 24.71% in Tower Hamlets. Two criteria were adopted as the basis for selection.

First, we attempted to reflect the different contexts in which counselling was provided within voluntary sector agencies. Accordingly, the agencies selected included two specialist counselling agencies dealing with relationship problems, three agencies supporting those with alcohol and drug dependency, two agencies supporting mental health sufferers, two women-only agencies with a broad social care remit, and a counselling and advisory service for young people. Second, wherever possible, we attempted to identify locations where we could 'match' agencies which were intended to serve the whole population with agencies which specifically catered to the needs of one or more minority ethnic groups, while dealing with similar issues. For example, in Leeds, we reviewed MIND and the Leeds Black Mental Health Forum (LBMHF) which both support people with mental health problems. For convenience, we refer to the former as mainstream agencies and the latter as black agencies. Accordingly, an equal number of mainstream and black-led agencies were selected.

In addition, we examined the policy and practices of three umbrella organisations with strategic responsibility for the planning and provision of counselling services. Two of these organisations were also responsible for providing training courses in counselling

# Appendix B: Interviewee profiles

| Profile of non-clients | | | | Profile of clients | | | |
|---|---|---|---|---|---|---|---|
| Pseudonym | Gender | Age | Ethnicity | Pseudonym | Gender | Age | Ethnicity |
| Sahila | F | 40 | Pakistani | Zabi | F | 24 | Pakistani |
| Bushra | F | 32 | Scottish-Pakistani | Munna | M | 44 | Pakistani |
| Aysha | F | 21 | Pakistani | Karima | F | 60 | Asian |
| Abdulah | M | 39 | Bangladeshi | Ali | M | 42 | Asian-Scottish |
| Mohammed | M | 52 | Indian | Nari | F | 53 | Indian |
| Memet | M | 52 | Muslim-Pakistani | Noori | F | 35 | Indian |
| Uma | M | 63 | Bangladeshi | Ram | M | 33 | Indian |
| Sima | F | 72 | Indian | Rani | F | 54 | Indian |
| Champa | F | 47 | Muslim | Shyam | M | 45 | Indian |
| Rasa | F | 50 | Pakistani | Gopal | M | 60 | Hindu |
| Radha | F | 57 | British-Indian | Rahim | M | 49 | Asian |
| Bees | F | 30 | Indian | Raj | M | 48 | Indian |
| Banoo | F | 37 | Bangladeshi | Mamta | F | 45 | Asian |
| Suki | F | 50 | Scottish-Sikh | Salma | F | 46 | Pakistani |
| Sakhi | F | 67 | East African | Asif | M | 61 | Pakistani-Scottish |
| Kaji | M | 75 | Asian | Khalid | M | 45 | Pakistani |
| Sharat | M | 54 | Hindu | Raksha | F | 46 | Scottish-Sikh |
| Bibi | F | 41 | Muslim | Shahida | F | 44 | Indian |
| Simeela | F | 59 | Pakistani-Asian-Muslim | Jasmin | F | 28 | Indian |

# Appendix C:
# Participating agencies

*Umbrella Organisations*  Relate Headquarters (Rugby)
          Westminister Pastoral Foundation (London)
          Alcohol Concern (London)

*Black agencies*     Leeds Black Mental Health Forum (Leeds)
          Meridian (Glasgow)
          Awaz Utaoh (Bristol)
          Asian Family Counselling Service (London)
          Ethnic Alcohol Counselling in Hounslow (London)

*Mainstream agencies*   MIND (Leeds)
          Bristol Drugs Project (Bristol)
          Glasgow Council for Alcohol (Glasgow)
          Tower Hamlets Youth Counselling and Advisory Service (London)
          Hounslow branch of Relate (London)